NOV 2 4 2014

W9-BXX-566

THE FEAR REFLEX

NOV 2 4 2014

THE
FEAR
REFLEX

5 WAYS TO OVERCOME IT AND
TRUST YOUR IMPERFECT SELF

>> <<

JOSEPH SHRAND, M.D.,
WITH LEIGH DEVINE

HAZELDEN®

Hazelden
Center City, Minnesota 55012
hazelden.org

© 2014 by Joseph Shrand and Leigh Devine
All rights reserved. Published 2014.
Printed in the United States of America

No part of this publication, either print or electronic, may be reproduced in any form or by any means without the express written permission of the publisher. Failure to comply with these terms may expose you to legal action and damages for copyright infringement.

Library of Congress Cataloging-in-Publication Data
Shrand, Joseph, 1958–
    The fear reflex : 5 ways to overcome it and trust your imperfect self / Joseph Shrand, M.D., with Leigh Devine.
        pages   cm
    ISBN 978-1-61649-554-1 (paperback)
    1. Fear.   2. Anxiety sensitivity.   I. Devine, Leigh, 1963–   II. Title.
    BF575.F2S473 2014
    152.4'6—dc23

                                                        2014024740

Editor's note
    The names, details, and circumstances may have been changed to protect the privacy of those mentioned in this publication. In some cases, composites have been created.
    This publication is not intended as a substitute for the advice of health care professionals.

17 16 15 14   1 2 3 4 5 6

Cover design: Jon Valk
Interior design: Terri Kinne
Typesetting: Bookmobile Design and Digital Publisher Services
Illustrations: Sophia Tyler Shrand
Figure 2 originally appeared in Outsmarting Anger: 7 Strategies for Defusing Our Most Dangerous Emotion by Joseph Shrand, M.D., with Leigh Devine (San Francisco: Jossey-Bass, 2013).
Figure 3 originally appeared in Manage Your Stress: Overcoming Stress in the Modern World by Joseph Shrand, M.D., with Leigh Devine (New York: St. Martin's Griffin, 2012).

To my wife, my partner, my Vitamin "C,"
my best friend, Carol. You are the one who has provided
the truest antidote to fear. I love coming home to you.

Contents

3 0053 01133 7097

Acknowledgments

I stand on the shoulders of giants and would like to acknowledge them and their inspiration.

Sid Farrar, my editor from Hazelden who believed in the I-M Approach from the minute he heard about it. His superb skill has helped craft the message and taken me and the book to another I-M!

Linda Konner, the best agent in the world, who put me in touch with Sid.

Jim Quine, my "brudder from anudder mudder" who grasped the power of the I-M Approach the first time he heard it about a decade ago and has used it ever since.

Avrom Weinberg, Ph.D., for pushing me to explain. He is very, very missed.

All of my clinical and support staff at CASTLE and who have embraced the I-M Approach as the foundation of treatment, demonstrating over and over the power of treating someone with respect.

Erich Englehardt, my student who continues to challenge me as we refine the I-M Approach and its application.

Jerry Fain, truly "faintastic," who prompted me to write essay after essay on the power of the Approach.

Julie Silver, M.D., my first editor at Harvard, without whom I would never have become a writer of books at all.

Tony Komaroff, M.D., who has championed getting the message of science into the hands of the general public.

Leigh Devine, M.S., my writer and friend, who has been able to always take our books to the next I-M.

Jeff Brown, Ph.D., who has inspired me beyond belief with his courage in the face of inconceivable challenge.

Charles Darwin, need I say more?

EO Wilson, right up there with Darwin.

Alan Watts, for introducing me to the western discovery of Buddhism and how connected all of us really are.

My parents, Hyman Shrand and Frances Shrand, who provided me with the education and support that have helped me to overcome my own fears.

My wife Carol's parents, Richard and Dorothy McCann, who helped bring into the world that one amazing, unique person who has never doubted me, and for all their love, support, and belief.

My sister Lana Maxwell, who never doubted me once—well, maybe just that once!

My departed sister Susan, who is now at her eternal I-M. I miss you.

My kids, Sophie, Jason, Galen, and Becca, who showed me how a child is always influenced by the four domains and how influential a parent can be in creating an environment in which a child can demonstrate who he or she is. This has been even more incredible than I could ever have imagined.

My sister-in-law Elizabeth St. Lawrence, who was one of the first people I ever showed the I-M Approach to way back when in 1982, a critical thinker who keeps me honest.

Daniel Mumbauer, president and CEO of High Point Treatment Center, who took a chance on me back in 2008 when he asked me to help design an adolescent addiction treatment program. His mission and that of the I-M Approach have always been in synchrony.

Fran Markle, vice president of High Point Treatment Center, who has given me the support I need to make a real difference in the lives of kids and their families challenged by addiction.

Larry Bosco, one of the most incredible therapists I know who has taken the I-M Approach and applied it for years, even after he left the hospital where we worked together. In fact, for a long time he was the only person I trusted to use the Approach without my direct supervision.

David Singer, a brilliant neuropsychologist who has debated with me the foundations and application of the I-M Approach, always making sense and helping to move to a deeper understanding and appreciation of the brain.

Mark Stiles, who wanted to finally be acknowledged for something and is now helping to "brand" the I-M Approach.

The hundreds of innovators and thinkers whose work has inspired me and been integrated into the I-M Approach.

And the thousands of patients who have helped me believe that a person who feels valued can heal the deepest wounds, creating battle scars of which they can be proud and feel no fear. They are truly the giants.

Introduction

"Because fear kills everything," Mo had once told her.
"Your mind, your heart, your imagination."

—**Cornelia Funke,** *Inkheart*

Sally was late for the team-building session. She stood shyly in the doorway to the gym, just as the group leader was telling the new employees to break up into smaller clusters to start the next exercise. She scanned the room. And there, on the farthest side of the gymnasium, she saw a guy from her office. A guy she had wanted to talk to for days. A guy she had been too timid to approach. A guy whom she liked, but thought would never like her. And there was an empty seat right next to him.

She froze with fear.

To her immediate left was an empty seat next to a woman she knew well. All she had to do was sit there and she would be part of a group. But Sally squelched the fear that had risen from her gut to her heart to her throat and took a step, then another, and walked across the room and said, "Is this seat taken?" "No, it's all yours. I'm Harry." And Sally sat down. She had taken the first step in overcoming fear.

I heard this story from a patient who had been struggling with insecurities that had crippled her in almost every aspect of her life: relationships, job advancement, trying new things, or going to new places. Sally was afraid she was not good enough for a relationship and not smart enough or capable enough to advance in her career, would fail if she tried something new, and was not bold enough to have an adventure. Sally felt imperfect, and that meant the world would see her as imperfect as well. Her fear had crippled her, freezing initiative, thwarting ambitions, draining desire, and dulling her dreams. Fear had left her paralyzed and robbed her of her capacity to explore her world.

Fear, like a screaming siren, can catapult us into action for the sake of life itself, just as someone shouting, "Run for your life!" or "Fire!!!" can clear a crowded area in a hot minute. Fear can also freeze us where we stand—the "deer-in-the-headlights" response. Flee or freeze: in a heartbeat, we can engage either response when faced with real and immediate danger. Fear, and our response to it, helped us survive in our ancestral prehistoric days as it does in our modern world today. There is nothing wrong with fear: it's what you do with it that can get you into trouble.

Our fear reflex can activate just as intensely when danger is not real at all but simply imagined. Imaginary dangers can make us run away from success toward a world of disappointment and unfulfilled dreams. They can grip the human psyche as strongly as a bear's embrace and paralyze a person as surely as fears of real dangers can, trapping a person somewhere between flight and fight and freeze. While appropriate and rational fear can be a lifesaver, irrational fear can stifle your creativity and stop your life in its tracks. That's what happened to Sally, who found herself unable to make a decision, unable to move or cross a gymnasium floor. Her fear was in control . . . at first.

Quite often, fear seems to punch us in the gut out of nowhere, triggered spontaneously with no apparent source. Irrational and relentless, fear propels us back into the deep, dark jungle of our evolutionary heritage—an unjustified terror based more on what we imagine than what is really occurring. Imaginary danger can paralyze us, as careers, relationships, and the joy and amazement of simply being alive fade further and further into the distance.

I see this every day in my practice as a psychiatrist. A middle-aged woman reluctant to ask for a raise out of fear that her boss might fire her. A divorced man afraid to enter a new relationship for fear he'll be rejected. A creative, talented teenager afraid to apply to his first-choice college because he believes he isn't good enough. A young child who is so sure of monsters in the closet that she dare not go to sleep.

Modern humans walking on earth today carry vestiges of fear formed over millions of years of evolution. As if we still lived in the wild and were protecting our territory, our fear reflex leaps from the same part of our brain—the limbic system—that once produced the reactions that protected us from a saber-toothed tiger or a venomous snake or a marauding member of a competing clan who is plotting to rob or kill us. Many people still live in a world fraught with fear, dread, terror, and worry over real threats to their lives. There are countries and neighborhoods where that terror is justified, where the safety of citizens may be at the whim of an authoritarian regime or gang, where unprovoked attacks are commonplace. But for many of us, even though we may live in safe homes and communities, our ancient heritage of fear can become a fact of daily life, causing us to act as if our basic survival is always in jeopardy.

Do any of these seem familiar to you? Fear of failure. Fear of success. Fear of not having enough or of losing what you have. Fear of germs. Fear of failing health or failing economies. Fear of strangers, being alone, commitment, or abandonment. Fear of crossing the street, or of someone crossing the street in your direction. Fear of flying, driving, dying—of life itself. You name it; our world is permeated with fears.

The very fabric of our daily lives is pervaded with images and sounds of terrifying events captured in the news or recreated as "entertainment" in countless movies, TV shows, and video games, then released like a maelstrom into our living rooms, bedrooms, offices, movie theaters, and even our cars. We are fed a steady stream of violence and revenge, with strangers attacking each other with roadside bombs, drones, knives, guns, bricks, or fists at the slightest provocation, as if this were the natural state of affairs. And even if we choose to get our information and entertainment through reading—whether books, newspapers, magazines, or browsing the Web—we can't escape the fearmongering that characterizes everything from editorials to celebrity exposés, and from political blogs to the pharmaceutical ads on your browser's home page. It is amazing we venture outside the safety of our homes at all into what is presented as such a dangerous and deadly world. Our fear reflex can seem to be on overdrive, as if around every corner we may encounter our modern-day equivalent of a saber-toothed tiger.

Fear stems from our inherent desire to survive and instills in us a growing sense of caution, which slowly increases as our brains shift us from being impulsive infants to adults who are able to anticipate the future. But ultimately, fear is the result of thinking our impulses and actions, or the impulses and actions of others, will result in harm. Like a driver on a road, we slow down at a caution sign, but stay immobile at a stop sign, red with the symbol of danger. As humanity has evolved, the fear reflex has been preserved to protect our survival and our species. Yet that same fear reflex today, paradoxically, can prevent us from living full lives.

But it doesn't have to. In this book, we'll explore fear as a reflexive mechanism inherited from our preverbal history, the underlying sources of fear in our modern-day world that trigger that reflex, and strategic ways you can modify your fear reflexes. I will offer you a road map to understand where your fear comes from and how to take the steps you need to overcome the debilitating effects of this most basic of emotions—just like Sally did when she walked across the room and sat next to Harry.

As a psychiatrist for more than twenty years, I have had unique access to what makes the human psyche tick, especially when it comes to fear. I work on a daily basis with people struggling to confront a myriad of fears. These modern-world fears are the shadows of the saber-toothed tigers, snakes, or marauding tribes that threatened early humans. There really is safety in numbers, and, like early humans who learned they needed to cooperate with each other to stand a chance against these material enemies, ultimately we can recognize these shadows as disguises for our imagined fear of being cast out of our protective group: alone, isolated, and having to fend for ourselves.

The power our modern fears have over us depends on our answer to this essential question: Do I have value? How we answer this profoundly influences all our actions. Will what we do cause us to be *de*-valued by the people who matter in our lives. People who believe they have little value to their protective group feel that they are at risk of being rejected, kicked out. With this at the heart of our myriad fears, we defend ourselves in many self-defeating ways—from suppressing our feelings and talents and doing nothing that will draw attention to our inadequacies, to acting out our fear with anger to push people away before they can reject us.

But as fearful as my patients may be, they have also taught me that within each of us lies the capacity to overcome our fears, no matter how deeply seated and irrational they are. The fear reflex can be recognized, controlled, and managed so that the safety, happiness, and success we all crave can be realized, each to our own capacity. I have written this book to share a remarkably simple yet powerful way to do just that, one that taps into the amazing innate abilities that are unique to each of us.

As you progress through the five ways to understand and address fear in this book—Tiny Terrors, Rapid Response, Unexpected Undercurrents, Social Security, and Traversing Together—I will show you how to reframe and contain your fears. By changing the way you perceive yourself and others, you will be able to overcome those fears and trust yourself as an imperfect human being.

I will help you create a shift in your life—one that you never thought would be possible.

I am going to teach you how to use an idea I developed over twenty years ago, which I use on a daily basis with my patients and apply in my everyday life. I developed this concept and treatment philosophy after many years of seeing most of the current behavioral health treatment methods fail miserably, not because of the techniques themselves, but because at their foundation is what I consider to be a fatal flaw: they put a label on people and call them "sick." Most psychological theories assume that labeling negative or maladaptive feelings and behaviors as pathologies so they can be studied and diagnosed like physical diseases is the key to helping people. We are taught to assume that a person is "broken" and needs to be fixed so they can do better. I am not convinced that label is useful in treating even severe psychiatric conditions that have a genetic or neurological variation requiring medical intervention; I believe this blanket pathologizing of challenging behaviors and painful emotions has been carried to an extreme and has become counterproductive.

My method challenges the very concept of "sickness," instead replacing it with the idea that we are all doing the best we can at this and every moment in time, with the potential to change from second to second in response to our internal and external environments. Change the environment, change the response.

I call my method the "I-Maximum" or "I-M Approach." I'll mostly use I-M (think "I AM!" when you say it) throughout this book for convenience.

In this book, I am going to teach you how to apply the I-M Approach to the fear reflex, but you can use it in practically every moment of every day to improve your life and the life of those around you. You can use this method to help you begin to really understand and trust who you are, and take control of where you want to go. I believe that everyone is at an I-M, a current maximum potential. And when you believe that as well, amazing things begin to happen.

The I-M Approach

Remember Sally from page one? For years, she had seen herself through a lens of not being smart enough, strong enough, pretty enough, good enough. And Sally's not alone. Many of us see ourselves through that lens. We ask, "What is wrong with me?" We feel broken and unsure of our value in the world. For Sally, this feeling held her back in relationships, career advancement, and enjoyment of life. Seeing herself as flawed was tantamount to seeing herself as a loser.

But I believe that Sally—and each of us—reacts and responds the best we can to the influence of the world around us, and the world within us—and that is the crux of the I-Maximum, or I-M, Approach.

What if we stop seeing ourselves as inadequate? What if, instead, we begin to look at ourselves as an I-M: **I am** at my **maximum,** doing the best I can in *this* situation, at *this* moment in time? The best Sally could do when she walked into the gymnasium was become afraid. But Sally had learned the I-M Approach and used it right there: instead of seeing herself as inadequate because of her fear, Sally knew she was at her I-M, even with her fear. She might not be perfect, but she was doing the best she could at that moment. She knew that she didn't have to like her I-M or condone it. But she knew her I-M was in her control, and she held herself responsible for it—which gave her power. So, rather than beat herself up about it, she instead *respected herself* as someone doing the best she could do at that moment, which made her ready to change to and respect whatever would be her next I-M. When was the last time you felt like a failure when someone treated you with respect?

You can't. And I think that has the same reliability as gravity.

Apples don't fall up and the brain does not generate negative feelings like fear and anger that tell you you're a failure when it feels respected. It just can't.

When we feel inadequate, like a failure, we get angry with ourselves a lot. Anger is the opposite of fear—it is the fight branch of the fight-flight-freeze response. Think about this for a moment: How do you feel around an angry person? Probably very anxious. This makes sense from an evolutionary point of view. Anger is an emotion designed to change the behavior of someone else, very often with the intention of getting that person to run away in fear. So what do you think happens to us when we get angry with ourselves? We can begin to fear ourselves, which leads to mistrusting and disrespecting ourselves. Is it any wonder that we then get stuck—frozen like a deer in our very own headlights!

The I-M Approach can change all that instantaneously. When Sally *respected* her I-M fearful self instead of getting angry with herself for being afraid, she could begin to move away from both anger and fear. Her anger never materialized because she was able to defuse it with self-respect, which allowed her to move through her fear, walk across that room, and meet the man she had wanted to talk with for a long time.

That is the whole basis of the I-M Approach, and Sally used it to reinterpret the fear that rose from her stomach to her heart to her throat as being the best she could be at that moment. That doesn't mean she *liked* or condoned her fearful self, but she could still respect herself and not let that part of her guide her actions. Even if her fear reflex compelled her to hide or take the safe alternative, by recognizing that this fear was her I-M, she was able to hold herself responsible for it. Taking that responsibility gave her the power to make a conscious decision and exercise control of her life by choosing a different I-M and walking across the room.

Fear is bred through a primitive worry that at any time we may be vulnerable to attack and won't be able to fend off danger.

As we've seen, this gets translated into the fear that we won't have the protection or acceptance of the group to which we desire to belong because we may not be good, or strong, or valuable enough. Adopting the I-M Approach changes all of that. You are *not* inadequate or broken: you are simply at an I-M, your "current maximum potential." At this moment in time (*current*), you are doing the best you can (*maximum*), but with the *potential* to change in the very next second. This concept does not mean your current I-M is the best you will ever do—it may not be. But then again, by allowing room to respect yourself and others for always being at their I-M, you're unlikely to choose to do *worse* than your current I-M. We may not like it, but we can respect it, and by respecting it, we have the power to move on.

We can also think of the word "respect" in another way by breaking it into two parts: "re" = again, and "spect" (as used in the word in*spect*) = look. Let's *look again* at why we are doing what we are doing, without judgment, but with wonder, curiosity, and interest. Re-spect. Look again. When we sharpen the focus through our new lens of perception, we remind ourselves of our own value, as well as the value of other people.

Respect leads to value, value leads to trust, and trust leads to acceptance. The I-M Approach allows us to trust and believe in our "imperfect" self, and others as valuable imperfect selves, based on the view that we are all doing the best we can at this and every moment in time, with the potential to change from second to second.

The Four Domains of the I-M Approach

One of my patients, Jimmy, is a great example of how fear can really get in your way. He had come to his first visit because he was afraid to go to school. Just talking about school made him tremble. Some kids were cruel to him at school, mocking him for being a "scaredy-cat" when he wouldn't stand up for himself, making his fear even worse. He knew they saw him as a loser, which made him feel like one, so why would he want to go to school to be reminded of that every day? Every morning at home, sitting at his kitchen table, he would shake, his Mom gently urging him to "Just try, honey. Today may be a better day. Try. What is there to be afraid of?" But Jimmy was afraid. He had missed so many school days he was in danger of repeating tenth grade. It was not so much the thought of failure that shook him, but the idea of his torture at school continuing relentlessly and endlessly, defining his high school experience. Tenth grade threatened to be the worst year of his life, which he was doomed to repeat until he graduated. He was paralyzed with fear and just could not leave

---

▶ **KERRI STRUG**

In the 1996 Summer Olympics, little gymnast Kerri Strug was a favorite to win gold in the women's all-around. The Russian competition was tough, and every point the team could eke out would help. Strug's teammate stumbled badly in the vault competition, and when Kerri went for her first run, she under-rotated the landing of her first attempt, causing her to fall and damage her ankle. Things weren't looking too good for the American women after that, but Strug still needed to make her second vault. Wincing, with her ankle now bandaged, she limped to the starting position. She had to land this vault perfectly in order for the United States to win. She focused intently, putting pain out of her mind, and she flew down the mat, leapt up onto the vault, flipped over in perfect formation, and landed impeccably.

Nobody expected Strug could do her best, let alone even try. But her 1-M of a sprained ankle did not daunt Kerri. Instead, with tremendous determination, she prevailed, clinching the gold for the United States. The rest, of course, is history.

home and go to school. As bad as this situation may sound, let's see what happens when we look at it from the perspective that this was his I-M.

Jimmy was doing his best, even while sitting in fear at his kitchen table. He was at his current maximum potential, even if he didn't like it or think it was OK. But his I-M did not happen in a vacuum. Everyone's I-M is influenced by four domains.

Two of these are inside our bodies: the *biological domain* of our brain and body, and a domain I call the "*Ic domain*," or *how I see myself and how I think other people see me.* Two domains are outside our bodies: our *Home* and *Social domains.* I will explore each of these domains in detail in the next several chapters, but here is a general overview of each and its influence on fear and the I-M.

The Biological Domain

Jimmy, Sally, and Kerri Strug were all influenced by their biological domains. Kerri's ankle had twisted in a way that ankles are not designed to twist. The muscle cells in her ankle responded the best they could, given the change in their environment: some tore while others may have cramped and constricted. To protect the bone and prevent further injury to the muscle, surrounding tissue probably swelled with water, creating a cushion designed to minimize further damage. But the swelling of that tissue placed a new pressure on the nerves of her ankle, causing pain and warning her brain that she had been hurt. Were any of those cells responding in a way that wasn't the best they could, given the fact that she had landed awkwardly on her ankle?

When Sally and Jimmy felt the fear rise from their gut, they became progressively paralyzed. While Sally used the I-M Approach to overcome it, Jimmy did not have those tools at this point in his story. Even so, Jimmy's body was responding the way a body should when confronted with a perceived threat to its very survival. His brain had activated its ancient fight-flight-freeze response as if there were a saber-toothed tiger roaming the hallways and class-rooms of his school.

From an evolutionary viewpoint, Jimmy was perfect. We've seen how the flight response has been well preserved in our human species as a critical tool in survival. Jimmy did just what he was meant to do if faced with a life-threatening danger: Jimmy's brain had perceived a threat, created a fear response, and got the rest of the body to do what it needed to do to survive another day. Be afraid, his brain told him, get away, and live. Don't go to school. Don't leave the house. Don't, don't, don't. But the only *real* danger was that Jimmy may have to repeat tenth grade. The biological domain is often the easiest for us to identify in ourselves because we feel its direct impact. In the next chapter, "Tiny Terrors," we'll explore exactly how to embrace your I-M in the biological domain.

The Ic Domain

The chapter "Rapid Response" explores the second internal domain called the "Ic" (pronounced "I see"), which refers directly to how you see yourself and, perhaps more importantly, how you think other people see you. Together they create the Ic: your current concept of yourself.

Human beings are interested in what other people think or feel. We call this "empathy." "How ya feelin'?" we ask. But what we are really interested in is, "What are you thinking or feeling about *me*?" This is not just empathy but something more. We assess ourselves through the eyes of others. The result of this assessment is embodied in the Ic domain.

Sally was worried the man across the room would see her as an undesirable partner, which had an influence on her Ic and sense of self. Jimmy worried he would be viewed as a loser by the other kids at school, and could not appreciate that his mom saw him differently. And Kerri Strug recognized that other people, in fact an entire country, saw her as their path to an Olympic gold medal.

In scientific circles, our human ability to appreciate another person's point of view goes by the rather forbidding term "Theory of Mind." These words are chosen to describe the amazing human ability to "theorize" what someone else is thinking or feeling, and being able to take someone else's perspective. I will explore the Ic domain and Theory of Mind in the chapter "Rapid Response."

The Home Domain

The first two internal domains, biological and Ic, are influenced by the third and fourth domains, the *home* domain and the *social* domain. These two domains are outside our bodies and refer to the attachments and relationships we make in the world.

I don't think anyone is going to deny that the home domain—that foundational place where many of our ideas, habits, and beliefs are formed—has an influence on our I-M, even in our adult lives. Yet, even when parents strive to help their children feel safe and sound, the home domain can bring with it an unexpected and unintended source of fear. In the chapter "Unexpected Undercurrents," we explore how each of us is programmed by the culture in which we live, starting with our upbringing, including our parents' fear impulses, and continuing all the way through adulthood. For instance, most parents inherently protect their children from harm, but may unwittingly be sending a subtle message to their kids that the world is unsafe. Perhaps a home has a massive number of locks on the doors and windows or a complicated alarm system, projecting a daily fear of intruders. Parents may tell their children not to wander around the neighborhood but stay close to home, even though the neighborhood is safe and other kids roam freely, having a good time together. Perhaps "helicopter parents" are sending a mixed message by hovering, unwittingly creating a dependency and sense of incompetency that may last long after childhood, as their adult children fear a dangerous world in which one needs to be protected.

And while I would never suggest that parents *not* be their children's guardians and neglect protecting them from real dangers, instilling in our children a sense of trust and independence is also critical to their development. Parents traverse the delicate tightrope of being overly protective and hovering versus trusting and empowering their children to manage the world around them. Home should be a place of safety, but also a place from which to safely venture out into the rest of the world and society.

This is not about blaming parents for the inadequacies of their kids, nor is it about giving parents too much credit for their kids' successes. The home domain is given a place of honor because it is such an influential foundation for so many of the choices we make later in life and in the rest of the world; but it is neither a panacea nor an immunization against the influence of the next external domain, the social domain.

The Social Domain

The things that happen at home influence the choices we make in the social domain, or the rest of the world in which we live. And the choices we make in the social domain then impact the choices we make back at home. These influences on our fear reflex are investigated in the chapter "Social Security." The social domain is everything in the external world other than the home domain. It's being at work, at school, on a date at a restaurant, at a bar with friends, or just walking down the street.

The relative safety of that social world, however, is also influenced by the way society and its inhabitants are presented by the media. We noted how electronic and print media create a culture of fear with their focus on violence, disease, and disasters. To the degree that we take in these messages and believe them, even unconsciously, our social domain will be characterized by fear and mistrust. You never know what may happen just outside your door. And perhaps we begin to wonder about our own neighbors.

Which means your neighbors may be wondering about you. Yes, our culture tells us to be afraid, be very afraid. Take these pills, don't eat this food, watch out for these people—maybe you ought to buy a gun. Our social domain has an enormous influence on our home, biological, and Ic domains, and the choices we make as we live our lives.

The Fear Reflex and the I-M Approach

Jimmy's story illustrates how the I-M Approach can serve as a road map for why we do what we do. And once we know the "whys" we have a better chance of changing our understanding of the world and our responses to that world, and we have more choices in that world.

Jimmy's biological and Ic domains were influenced by his so-cial domain in the sixth grade: he saw another girl throw up in the classroom. Now, the transition to sixth grade can be fear provok-ing as it is; most kids in the United States move from the close and cozy confines of a safe, single elementary school classroom to the harrowing halls of a large middle school. They have to figure out where to go for English and math, but also decipher myriad complex relationships with peers, teachers, and administrators. School can be a tough social domain to navigate.

Already feeling a little anxious, Jimmy was sitting in the back of the class when it happened. A girl two rows ahead of him sud-denly raised her hand. The teacher was writing on the board, and the flailing hand of despair was not immediately noticed.

From his vantage point, Jimmy saw the entire process unfurl. The girl ahead of him began to desperately ask for the teacher's at-tention. The teacher, her back turned, told the girl to wait a minute and continued writing the homework assignment on the board. Jimmy watched as the student's other hand rose rapidly toward her mouth. The girl stopped talking. Her raised hand dropped to cup the other already over her mouth. In a fluid motion, the girl fumbled to stand, the teacher turned, and the first visible vomit began to emerge from around the student's hands. The girl began to run to the classroom door; the teacher looked on, astonished, while the rest of the kids began to laugh or gag, or look disgusted. Jimmy, in the back row, looked on in horror.

His nightmare had begun. Jimmy knew that for the rest of this girl's life at school, she would be known as the kid who threw up in Mrs. Bannister's science class. Jimmy's biological and Ic domains went wild. What if he threw up in class as well? What if he suffered the same humiliation?

In that moment, all four domains were interacting. All of the people in Jimmy's story were at their I-M. The teacher's Ic domain ignored the protestations of the girl, instead continuing to write the homework on the board, influenced by the expectation of members in her social domain: students, parents, her department head, her principal. That little girl's biological domain was doing the best it could to rid her stomach of whatever toxic substance was in there. And that one small event had an influence on Jimmy's I-M, and the I-Ms of all the other students, who would tell their friends, and leave the unfortunate girl with the Ic (how she sees herself) in the social domain of school as the girl who threw up in Mrs. Bannister's class.

Jimmy's social domain of school had influenced his biological domain, as his brain and body activated a new fear of throwing up in public. This fear then had an influence on his Ic domain, as he worried how other kids would see him. And this fear in the social domain influenced him to seek shelter in his home domain, but at the expense of venturing out into the world. His inertia at home then had an influence on the way he responded biologically, perpetuating his Ic sense of inadequacy, and leading him to avoid even further his foray out of the home and into the social domain.

The four domains of the I-M Approach are always fluidly inter-acting, and as they change, they influence the response of your I-M. As your I-M changes, it influences your response to the rest of the world. The I-M Approach can be graphically illustrated like this:

FIGURE 1
The I-M Approach

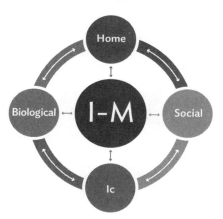

As our I-M changes, it influences the choices we make in any of the domains, and as the domains change, they influence our I-M—our current maximum potential. Always changing, but always in balance, I call this a "dynamic equilibrium." Each of us is always at an I-M.

The I-M Approach suggests that, as each of us is doing the best he or she can at any moment in time, each of us is worthy of respect. It's important enough to say again: respecting some-thing and liking something are two different things. But when we view each other through an I-M perspective, amazing things begin to happen.

Kerri Strug faced her fear and won an Olympic gold medal. Sally faced her fear and created an opportunity for a new relationship.

Jimmy's I-M was to remain in fear, but his fear persisted because he could not embrace his imperfect self, instead fearing he would be systematically rejected. Jimmy, like the rest, always has the potential to recognize and respect his I-M and move to the next I-M that may lead him back to facing his fears at school. We all have that potential: it's an I-M thing.

1

Tiny Terrors

The Biological Domain

"The oldest and strongest emotion of mankind is fear."
—H.P. Lovecraft

There was no question—Alan had heard a noise. At first he thought perhaps it was the water pipes. As part of his brain began coaxing him back to sleep, he heard it again—a subtle clink, a tap, a noise that was not there before and was not meant to be there at all. His entire body went on alert, starting with a surge of that most unpleasant feeling we get when startled. Someone, an intruder, was in his house.

Alan's fear was the result of millions of years of evolution. Our internal biological domain has been exquisitely honed over our evolution to rapidly discern even the tiniest changes in our surroundings. Starting almost as a newborn babe, our brains are drawn to differences, comparing sets of information without any conscious effort at all. Newborn babies will shift their gaze to a line drawn across a blank page. They are interested in the difference between the dark line that has divided the page from a whole to separate parts. Newborn babies will startle and cry at the sound of a loud noise or a rapid change in position. They will activate the fear reflex. This ability has enormous survival potential: early humans who reacted to the rustling of a bush survived more often than those who ignored the potential warning sign of a predator. Our brains are adapted to compare and respond.

Alan's brain was no different. A change had occurred in his environment—a new sound—and that change scared him as his imagination began to consider the myriad of possible dangers. Not until later, when Alan gathered the courage to venture outside his room and downstairs, did he find his cat, up on the kitchen counter, focused on tapping one metal bowl against another. Sometimes we can be fooled by fear.

The Basic Brain

The activation of our fear reflex starts with this perception of difference. Whether danger is real or imagined, the biological response is initially the same. To appreciate this remarkable cascade, it is important to understand a bit more about our amazing brain.

One of my favorite books is *The Accidental Mind* by David Linden.[1] Linden suggests that during the evolution of our brain, we never threw anything away; we just built one chunk of brain on top of the other. The result can be thought of as a three-scoop ice-cream cone.

The Brain Stem

The first scoop is the brain stem, often called the "reptilian" or "lizard" brain, which is responsible for most automatic things we don't even think about. Breathing, heart rate, and the regulation of many body systems are the responsibility of the brain stem. Without it we would not be able to breathe and the result would be death.

FIGURE 2

The brain as a three-scoop ice-cream cone

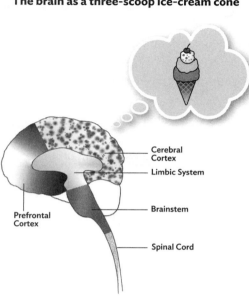

The Limbic System

The Limbic System

During evolution, animals began to rely on more than just the brain stem for survival. As more and more creatures emerged, some were small, others large. Some ate only select foods while others ate whatever they could find. Hundreds of millions of years ago, in order to survive in this growing world of complexity, animals developed a very simple and efficient response to other animals: the fight-flight response. We talked in the introduction about how this internal response to a change in the external world was so successful that we conserved it from one generation to the next. Our human brain still responds reflexively to the perception of a threat, just like Alan did to the unfamiliar sound. Fear is an avoidance emotion that drives our body to protect ourselves or flee, get away, escape.

The part of the brain responsible for this primitive fight-flight reflex sits on top of the brain stem: the limbic system. The limbic system is a complicated interconnection of brain structures that, combined, looks like a ram's horns wrapping around the top of the brain stem. One part in particular called the "amygdala" seems responsible for impulses, for emotional memory, and is the seat of feelings and the seven basic emotions of anger, contempt, disgust, happiness, sadness, surprise—and fear. It is in the amygdalae of our limbic system where fear originates, lives, and can fester.

It has a powerful role and a powerful influence on the choices we make and the fear we feel. Just the sound of something that was not meant to be there activated Alan's limbic system, which sent a message to the rest of his brain and body: Watch out. Danger.

The Neocortex

But our brain evolution did not stop there. We built the third scoop of the ice-cream cone right on top of the limbic system. This new brain, or neo (new) cortex (brain), consisting of the prefrontal and cerebral cortexes, truly distinguishes us as higher mammals. Different parts of the neocortex are responsible for different functions. For example, the back of the brain is responsible for processing visual information transmitted from the eyes. The top of the brain is responsible for moving our muscles. And the front of the brain, in particular the part just before the very front, is responsible for thinking, processing information, solving problems, executing a plan, and anticipating what will happen next. It is also the site of Theory of Mind, which we mentioned earlier and which will be the focus of the next chapter on the Ic domain.

We will spend a lot of time focusing on this part of the brain, called the "prefrontal cortex," or "PFC." The I-M Approach accesses the rational skills of the PFC to contain irrational limbic fears like Alan felt in the middle of the night, that Jimmy felt about school, and that Sally felt as she stood in the doorway of the gym.

The Fear Reflex

We have all felt afraid. Each of us can remember a time, perhaps even today, when even a small but sudden change in our environment made us startle. I felt my heart jump when a car pulled out a little too far from a driveway as I was approaching down the road. My sudden increase in heart rate was one of several remarkable bodily responses designed to save my life from a perceived threat. Everything that happened after my brain perceived that sudden change in my environment was designed to save my life. My I-M had changed, and my biological domain responded at a new current maximum potential.

Hiding from a predator is a great strategy. In essence, our body freezes; we become very, very quiet and hope the danger passes. But, once detected, that strategy stinks! Staying in one spot just makes you an easier target, and an easy and tasty snack. Rather than wait to be detected, the most important thing you can do to get away from a predator is . . . to run!!! That's where the flight branch jumps into play. I couldn't hide from that car pulling out in front of me. I had to do something else to survive.

Here is what happened in my brain and body, and what happens in all of us when we feel afraid. From that initial tiny terror, a cascade of physical events took place. My brain sent a messenger scientists call "ACTH" (adrenocorticotropic hormone) to the adrenal glands, two almond-shaped structures that live on top of the kidneys. My adrenal glands released adrenaline and cortisol, two ancient chemicals that began to work on other parts of my body. If you think back to those times you've been afraid, you will recognize these symptoms—changes in your body that seem distinct but are happening almost simultaneously. What is cool is that each has a really good evolutionary purpose, ultimately trying to save you from being eaten by a predator.

In order to run away, you have to get more energy to the muscles of your legs and arms. Our bodies use oxygen as a way to extract energy from the foods we eat, so to get more energy it makes sense that we would need more oxygen. To get more blood to the muscles of your legs and arms, your heart has to beat faster. So the first thing that happens when your brain activates the flight response is the release of adrenaline and cortisol, which increases heart rate and changes breathing.

Blood is pumped out of the heart into blood vessels of the circulatory system, our arteries and veins—basically a series of tubes that circulate blood throughout the body. These tubes start out like large water pipes, but get narrower and narrower. The faster the heart beats, the quicker it pumps the blood through your body to all the places it is needed. The tubes themselves narrow even more and constrict, increasing the blood pressure in those vessels. With that much pressure, the blood moves faster to the muscles of the arms and legs.

All that extra blood has to come from somewhere. Blood is diverted from the gut, as there is no point digesting lunch if you are about to be lunch. The unfortunate result may be nausea or "butterflies in your stomach." Blood is also diverted from the skin, resulting in the cold sweats; if you are going to run away from a predator, you may need to run fast and far. Cooling your skin decreases the chances of overheating in your race to escape. Brilliantly designed for survival, these symptoms of fear can be remarkably uncomfortable. In a way, that discomfort also propels us to do something: to get away from not only the predator, but those awful feelings. The brain and body are going to do what the brain and body are going to do. In an instant, they have moved from one I-M to a different current maximum potential, the best our brains and bodies can do in response to a change in our external environment. (See figure 3.)

All of these responses happened in Jimmy, in Alan, and in Sally, and happen in most of us when we experience fear. Their adrenal glands released a flood of adrenaline and cortisol. Their

FIGURE 3
The fear response

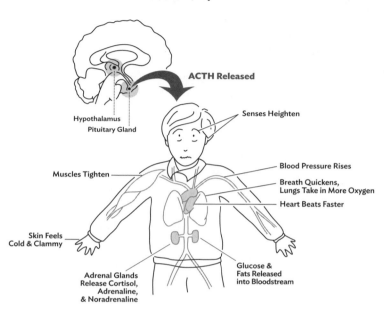

heart rate and blood pressure increased. Their breathing quickened. Their stomach began to flip over, and their skin became clammy with the cold sweats. Their thoughts were flooded with catastrophe, which fueled the fear itself, perpetuating the brain's bombardment of danger, danger, danger! For Jimmy in particular, the feeling of nausea was the worst thing possible, as it increased his belief that he was going to throw up.

What is remarkable is that Alan, Sally, and Jimmy all experienced basically the same fear reflex, which makes sense, since we have all evolved basically the same brain. But check this out: Alan's fear reflex was activated by a sound. Sally's fear reflex was activated by the sight of all those people in the gym. And Jimmy's fear reflex was activated by his *imagination*. Just the *idea* of going to school, not even actually being in the school, activated his fear reflex as efficiently as if there were a saber-toothed tiger growling right next to him. This is how powerful our limbic system can be, but that also has its own I-M. The limbic system, our adrenal glands, our heart and lungs and muscles are simply doing the best they can at that moment in time.

The biological domain demonstrates an important principle of the I-M Approach: *small changes can have big effects.* This is a critical insight when we begin to overcome the fear reflex. We don't have to do everything at once. If we think we have to change everything, we may get overwhelmed, which compounds our fear. The four domains are interconnected, and a small change in any one domain can have a ripple effect through the entire system. When Alan heard that noise in the dark, it began a cascade of events: a small change had a big effect. And when he saw his cat, that small change relaxed his fear. Even still, it took him a while to calm himself enough to fall back to sleep, as cortisol levels in his blood naturally reregulated.

The Nose Knows

Each of our senses can communicate fear. We see a scary movie we get scared. We hear a scary sound, we get scared. We feel something crawling on our skin, we get scared. And if we smell a smell associated with fear—that's right, our brain activates fear.[2]

The smell of fear is real. In a truly remarkable experiment, a team of scientists from the Netherlands showed men some very scary movies and then collected their sweat. All the men had followed a strict protocol for two days prior to watching the movie. The men were not allowed to drink alcohol; eat foods like onions, garlic, and asparagus; engage in any sexual activity; or exercise excessively. They were only allowed to use scent-free shampoo, soap, and deodorant given to them by the researchers. Before they entered the lab, they had to put on special T-shirts to prevent any odor contamination from their clothes. Once in the lab, they rinsed and dried their armpits with water and paper towels. Then an examiner, wearing special gloves to avoid any bacterial contamination, taped sterile absorbent gauze to their armpits. The men put on a new sterile T-shirt and were ready to begin the experiment.

After such a rigorous protocol, the scientists felt certain that the odor from these guys was not contaminated by anything that could alter the smell of their sweat. The volunteers then watched a scary movie, after which the gauze under their armpits was collected by the dedicated scientists. New gauze was put on, and the men then watched a neutral movie—a BBC documentary about Yellowstone National Park. The gauze samples were collected again, and this process was repeated, alternating between scary and neutral movies. The scientists were confident that any chemcals in that sweat had been influenced by the movie.

Then, the scientists took the sweat samples and asked the women participants to take a whiff. In a gesture that truly demonstrates a dedication to science, those women did what most women usually avoid, and then filled out a questionnaire. Now if you or I were asked to smell some sweaty stuff, we would probably wrinkle our noses in disgust. And that's exactly what the women did when exposed to the sweat generated by men watching movies about Yellowstone National Park. I mean, sweat smells pretty disgusting even in the best of times!

But when the women smelled the sweat produced from the scary movies, they made faces, not of disgust, but of fear. Their eyes widened, their noses flared, not wrinkled, and they looked afraid. Even though they had nothing to fear, they actually smelled the fear experienced by the men.

The Dutch scientists' experiment suggests that the ability to send an olfactory signal to our tribe mates alerting them to danger was a very useful survival tool. Imagine being in the dark, getting scared, but not wanting to make any noise that would

▶ DIS-ODERANT AND DAT-ODERANT

I wonder if our use of so many deodorants has had an impact on these subtle signals. Perhaps that's why they are so popular among young men and women trying to entice the other into a romantic relationship. The unconscious smell of fear is quite a deterrent, because a fearful person may not be one whom you would turn to for protection in a time of danger, and such a person would, therefore, be deprived of mating and getting their genes into the next generation. In this way, our biological domain directly interferes with our social domain, and produces a masked message to the Ic (the "I See" domain, i.e., how you see yourself and how you think others see you) of our prospective romantic relationship. Something smells fishy! Or not!

I also wonder if all of these marketing-driven scents have added to our communication problem. Olfaction research suggests we have retained our evolutionary propensity for these odiferous cues, and if they are being masked by deodorants, perfumes, and scented soaps, how are we meant to access the subtle, unconscious cues produced by our sweat? Granted, our brain is very dependent on auditory and visual cues, and we are nowhere near as adept at using smell to guide us as, say, our pet dog is. But the brain is still the brain, and those parts dedicated to olfaction are still integrated into the overall message delivered by our limbic system to our PFC for analysis. Now, I am not suggesting we go au naturel, but let's stop to think for a minute how our social domain has subtly enhanced our fear response. If we cannot tell what someone else is thinking and feeling, we are going to get naturally anxious. So if we are going to cover up this source of olfactory information, we may need to compensate by getting much better at communicating clearly with our verbal abilities.

attract the potential predator to you. Sending off a silent signal (not the same as an SBD—Silent But Deadly, a slang reference to flatulence!) would be a brilliant way to let your tribe mate know that danger was lurking nearby.

Fear and Disgust

When our fear response is mobilized, our bodies give off a distinct chemical signal, invisible to the eye, silent to the ear, but unconsciously picked up by our nose. The technical term for this is a "pheromone," a smell given off by one animal that triggers a response in another animal of the same species. In fact, the smell of fear causes us to increase our sniff response and scan our environment for the source of danger.

In a study out of Rice University in Texas, scientists had women perform a word-association task while being exposed to different smells: fear sweat, neutral sweat, and a control odor. The women who were smelling fear performed the word task more accurately without any slowing down of their response.[3] This makes sense, as being afraid in a situation demands a clear head and an ability to make decisions designed to help you survive. Fear itself is not a bad emotion to experience, and the Texas study suggests that even if you are not afraid, but around another person who is, you think more clearly.

Disgust can also be picked up without visual or auditory cues, in this case causing us to sniff less (that makes sense!), increasing our ability to see a target, and *decreasing* eye scanning.[4] Once we know where the source of disgust resides, we want to keep an eye on it, perhaps to back off if it starts to approach. The smell of fear elicits a logical and different response; we want to increase our ability to detect the source and keep looking around until we see it.

Both fear and disgust have enhanced our survival, and while both lead to an avoidance behavior, they just "feel" different, don't they? You know what it is to be fearful of and what it is to feel disgusted by a person. The first is attributed to a person who may hurt you, the second perhaps to a person who may infect you. We feel disgust when we see someone with poor hygiene, who looks dirty and smells dirty, but we don't automatically fear them. We probably want to avoid them to avoid being contaminated, not because we are afraid of being assaulted.

Fear of Infection

Fear of big things like toothy predators is relatively easy to understand, even for young children. But most humans today face tiny yet equally deadly threats: germs and parasites. Armed with caution and fear, we act in defense of acquiring these smallest of dangers on a daily basis by washing our hands, sanitizing, gargling, you name it. A fascinating theory introduced by evolutionary biologists suggests that our very emotions evolved as an adaptation to protect us from these tiny threats, with fear being one of the earliest emotions to emerge.[5]

Long before we knew about these microscopic creatures, our bodies developed a way to protect ourselves against bacteria and viruses: the immune system. Specialized blood cells send a message that an incursion has occurred; other blood cells are then recruited like soldiers in an army brigade to come and attack, defending our bodies against the invading germs.

Some scientists have even proposed that fear can mobilize the immune system. This idea is not so farfetched, as we know that part of the stress response is to get the immune system ramped up to protect against possible infection in case you are bitten by a predator. In fact, a recent study conducted by researchers at Trnava University in Slovakia suggests that just looking at pictures of things that could lead to disease is enough to get the immune system activated. Even more interesting is the cultural component. People from cultures where infectious diseases occur more frequently had higher immune response to those same pictures than people from countries where infectious diseases are less likely to occur.[6]

This is a wonderful example of how the human body reacts and adapts to survive its immediate surroundings—an evolutionary strength. But this also shows how our social domain has an influence on our biological domain. The immune systems of those from disease-prone countries are at a different level of functioning than those from less disease-prone countries, but both are at their own I-M. Fear can have an effect on how our immune system responds, something that is truly out of our conscious control. And yet, in an elegant survival dance that has been going on for millions of years, the biological domain of our bodies responds. The implication of this study is quite profound when we think about the subtle, and not so subtle, fears presented to us through the media. From the threat of halitosis (bad breath) to a disturbed night's sleep from coughing due to a cold, our brains are bombarded with the threat of illness, subliminally keeping us in constant fear.

Mirroring Fear

I once watched a movie in which a beautiful woman, in slow motion, bit into a peach. The juice squirted everywhere and, within milliseconds, I could feel my own mouth watering. I'm sure you've experienced something like this—pickles are especially effective in eliciting this response. Or perhaps you've seen someone look afraid and begun to feel a little scared yourself, maybe you even looked around for danger? These unconscious habits are actually abilities hardwired into our brains, through brain cells called "mirror neurons." Their discovery by Italian scientists is fairly recent.

In 1996 a team of researchers from the University of Parma, Italy, published a groundbreaking article with the catchy title

"Action Recognition in the Premotor Cortex." At the top of the brain is a section responsible for movement, called the "motor cortex." The scientists took two macaque monkeys and recorded the electrical activity of 532 neurons in their brains, located just in front of the motor cortex: the *pre*motor cortex. The monkeys being examined were strapped down so they could not move their arms or legs. They were then shown another monkey grabbing for a banana. The premotor cells went wild. It was as if the observing monkeys were getting ready to grab a banana themselves, even though they could not move their actual arms. Their brains were "mirroring" the movement of the other monkey.[7] This makes sense from an evolutionary perspective. If another monkey is going to gain an advantage by eating a banana, the observing monkey would want to prepare to do the same, so as not to miss out on a source of food.

We now know that mirror neurons are not just activated by movements like eating peaches or bananas. Mirror neurons also get activated by someone else's feelings. You see someone sad, you may feel sad. You see someone happy, you may feel happy. You see someone scared, you may feel scared; your own mirror neurons have been activated. In fact, we mirror a scared face within a second of seeing one![8] Mirror neurons are a remarkable biological response to the fear we see in those around us, and like so many of our biological systems, it has been honed to protect our survival.

Remembering Fear

Memory plays a crucial role in fear. We are naturally going to fear something in the present that posed a threat to us in the past, such as sounds, smells, and various experiences. But to demonstrate how our memories orchestrate our fears, I have to first explain a few terms frequently used in psychology circles. The first term is "unconditioned" and the second term is "conditioned." A new experience that results in fear is called an "unconditioned" response—we have never been in the situation or had the experience, but it scares us. We remember it for the next time. When confronted with a similar event, the PFC and limbic system have a quick chat. The limbic system accesses its memory banks, then sends a message to the PFC: "This was dangerous before and scared us." The PFC then makes an executive decision about how to react to the conditioned response—probably get the heck out of there! In this way, we respond immediately with fear; we have been conditioned.

▶ **LIFELONG FEAR IMPRESSIONS**

Tiny terrors may produce tiny responses, as in our need to use hand sanitizers on ourselves and our kids. But a traumatic event implies something so out of the norm that our brains respond with a cataclysm of fear. This fear can last a lifetime, dwelling in our memory the way a protective fear is supposed to, but often manifesting in detrimental ways, such as applying it when it's not needed. Some people who have experienced the trauma of war, of rape, or of being a first responder to a horrific event may jump and startle at sounds that another person may not even notice. In psychiatry, we have labeled this condition "post-traumatic stress disorder" or "PTSD"—stress lingers after (post) the traumatic event has long passed. Sleep does not come easy for folks with PTSD, for how is a brain supposed to sleep if it has to be on guard in the night? But from an I-M perspective, this is not a *disorder* at all, but a heightened, albeit misattributed, reaction of our brain and body—a reaction of the biological domain to an assault that may have occurred at home or in the social domain.

——————— Exercise ———————

FACE THE FACTS!

Have you ever wondered how you can "feel" something isn't right without really knowing why? We call this "intuition" or "instinct," that wordless, preverbal sense that something is wrong. For this we can thank our ancient limbic system and its cache of emotions, impulses, and memories. The amygdala, the core of the brain's limbic system, in particular plays a pivotal role in our ability to recognize a fearful face.[9] The facial display of fear crosses every culture worldwide: raised eyebrows, wide eyes, and flared nostrils. We recognize that another person is afraid, because we can access our own memory of what that emotion feels like. Mirror neurons prompt our facial muscles to consider moving like the other person's. But our ability to figure out what that person is thinking or feeling is part of our PFC, and Theory of Mind.

Try this today with a friend, your partner, your parent, or your kids. Make a sad face and ask them to guess what you are feeling. Make an angry face, a disgusted face, a scared face. I bet they can guess them all, even though you have not said a word! Now ask them to do the same: make a facial expression without telling you what the face is meant to represent. I bet you guess them all as well. Now try to reflect on what part of the face you actually looked at to get the most information. It will probably turn out to be the eyes.

You have used your PFC and Theory of Mind to figure this out. Interestingly, my patients with Asperger's syndrome, a form of autism, have some difficulty with this task. It is hard for them to identify what another person is thinking or feeling. And if you ask them what part of the face they would look at to figure out what another person *is* thinking or feeling, very often they will say the mouth, "Because that's where the words come from."

—————————————————————————

The Double Edge of the Fear Reflex

Our instant fear reflex was indeed useful when confronted with a life-threatening danger in the jungle or savannah, but it is significantly less helpful today on a crowded subway or just walking down the street. Imagine how our lives would be if we lived in fear all the time. For many people, unfortunately, that is exactly what is happening on a deep and unconscious level. You no doubt have people in your life whom you find jumpy, anxious, mistrustful, or afraid of their own shadow. You may be this way yourself to some degree. People in this state are always tiptoeing on the edge of fear. Rather than immediately regarding these behaviors or people in a negative light, it's more helpful to simply see this as their biological I-M. As we learned from Sally's and Kerri Strug's stories, the I-M is subject to change, if a person is of a mind to do so.

Fears, particularly the kind that plague us the most in this modern world, are based on the anticipation of an event. Memory is about the past, but anticipation is about the future. And anticipation is a function of the PFC. We are always fluidly, unconsciously assessing risk. Do I raise my hand and say the answer? Do I ask that boy or girl out? Do I apply for that new job? When we decide that the risk outweighs the potential benefit, we do not raise our hand, do not ask the boy or girl out, and perhaps play it safe and not fill out the job application.

In my field of psychiatry, this freeze response can progress to its most striking and intense form: catatonia. These folks have literally shut down and stopped moving! They sit or lie immobile, staring into space, unreachable. The catatonia may be accompanied by what we call "waxy flexibility" in which the arms and legs of the catatonic person can be moved by an observer and placed in a position, say with the left arm raised and the right arm straight out. Patients will retain this position for hours if not moved back to their original stance. Some theorists suggest this is a vestige of an ancient response to an encounter with a carnivore: freezing, pretending you were dead, and hoping the danger would pass.[10] I mention it here because it is such an extreme example of how fear can truly immobilize us.

In the introduction to this book, we met a boy named Jimmy who decided not to take a risk because of irrational fear of vomiting in school after seeing another classmate do so. That fear influenced his choice to stay home from school, but this decision came with an enormous number of other consequences. He was marked absent again and again, risking being held back in tenth grade. He missed a crucial test, risking having to take summer school. His mother and father were angry with him, as his fear was becoming an embarrassment to them, as well as a concern. They threatened to take away his cell phone and computer, because if he were going to stay home, he wasn't going to be texting friends or playing computer games.

His choice to stay home was an I-M influenced by the four domains. But that current maximum potential caused him to miss out on the little redheaded girl who actually really liked him and was hoping he would ask her to the tenth-grade social. This is the down side of fear: inhibiting us, freezing us, depriving us of moving to a different I-M.

Jimmy's limbic system was in control of his decisions, overriding his PFC's ability to anticipate what would happen if he continued to be overwhelmed by his fear. This was not a moral failing, but an I-M influenced by his biological domain. What small change could Jimmy make in any of the other domains to influence his I-M?

When it comes to fear, the limbic system is impulsive and reflexive, not thoughtful and reflective. If we do not mobilize our cortex, in particular the PFC, we can act impulsively on an intuition without the added benefit of anticipating the consequence of that action. Just think about what happens when someone shouts

▶ THE FOUR Rs

You might have seen this printed on a T-shirt, but it's absolutely true: what you think affects what you feel. This is the foundation of a therapy technique called "cognitive-behavioral therapy" or "CBT." CBT is a great way to reduce the symptoms of anxiety and to decrease fear. The goal is to shift control of your brain away from the limbic system to the PFC. Change what you think, change what you feel.

While there are many ways to do CBT, I use what I call "The Four Rs": recognize, rate, remember, reflect. The first step is to recognize that you are feeling anxious. The biggest mistake people make when they first feel anxiety is to pretend it's not there and try to distract themselves. This is what fear is all about: trying to get away, in this case from the anxiety itself. But this creates a huge problem. When you try to avoid your anxiety, you are creating a conditioned response. You are teaching your brain that you are not strong enough to deal with anxiety. Now if you don't think you are strong enough to deal with something, what happens to anxiety? It goes up and then you try to avoid it again, leading to a vicious and fruitless cycle. So the first step in managing your anxiety is to recognize you are anxious. "Ah," you can say to yourself, "I know what this is. It's anxiety." Recognition is a thinking function, so right away you have begun the shift to your PFC.

Recognizing anxiety is a reflective check-in on your reflexive biological response. Notice your heart beating faster, a change in your breathing, feeling sick to your stomach, or getting the cold sweats. Recognize that your muscles are tensing, you may start pacing, and you may begin to look around for danger and a way out. All of these biological responses are an activation of the flight branch of the fight-flight response: you are preparing to run away from a saber-toothed tiger, in spite of the fact that there isn't actually one present.

The second R is rate: rate your anxiety between 1 and 10,

with 10 being the most horrible panic you may have experienced, the worst fear you have ever felt. Rating is also a thinking function, once again moving your brain toward PFC control. Notice I don't say to rate yourself between zero and 10. Human beings are never at a zero. We are always at a low-grade anxiety called "vigilance." It is about survival. It is being able to distinguish the rustling in the bush that may mean a predator, or being aware of your surroundings when driving or crossing a road. Human beings are not designed to have no fear at all, as fear itself is protective. It is what we do with our fear that can get us in trouble. I have never had a patient give a rating of 10 when I asked the person to do this step. He or she may have been at a 10, but sitting in my office in relative safety, the person is not activating panic mode.

This leads to the third R: remember. Remember that anxiety is like a wave: it goes up but always comes down—always. You have just proved it by assigning this current anxiety a rating, distinguishing it from previous states. My guess is that you, the reader, also will not rate yourself at a 10. Memory is a function that links up the limbic system and the PFC. Once you remember that anxiety *always* goes away, what do you think happens to your anxiety? It decreases right then and there, because what you think affects what you feel.

Now you come to the fourth R, arguably, the most difficult: reflect. What was I thinking to begin with that made me so reflexively fearful? For every thought that makes you anxious, you can construct an opposite thought to decrease anxiety and the fear that feeds it. Every time. I once had a patient who worried about dying. "Dr. Shrand," he would say, "I know I'm going to die. You know I'm going to die. What's the opposite thought to that?" "Well," I said in my best psychiatrist voice, "If you're thinking about it, you're not dead." Every time he thought about dying he actually confirmed being alive.

When you use the Four Rs it is very important to do them

in order. Recognize, rate, remember, reflect. And write down those reflections. You have just taken control of your fear. But remember that even when you were afraid, that was your current maximum potential, your I-M.

"Fire!" in a crowded movie theater. The limbic system will mobilize faster than the PFC, which means you may be on your feet looking at the faces of others, quickly scanning the room, sniffing for smoke, before your PFC rationalizes that it was the guy at the back laughing and making an idiot of himself.

Keep it Frontal: Don't go Limbic

In an effort to help alleviate Jimmy's growing fears, his parents started bringing him in for consultation. Eventually, a small change occurred in therapy as we reviewed the Four Rs, and bumped up his Prozac, which helped change the internal environment of his biological domain. Another small change happened at home, as his parents reassessed their frustration and remembered that this was Jimmy's current I-M—that he wasn't skipping school on purpose or to annoy and embarrass them, but truly had a fear of being publically humiliated.

By not taking away his cell phone, they kept him in contact with the outside world and the little redheaded girl in particular. Another small change for Jimmy began with a shift in his social domain when that same girl texted him the English homework due the following week. In fact, she came over that night and revealed that she, too, once had a fear of going to school, and could completely understand why he kept staying home. Her ability to overcome her own fear was inspirational, activating Jimmy's mirror neurons in the biological domain, as well as helping him see himself as capable and able through his Ic domain.

Jimmy started using the I-M Approach and began to respect his fear: re = again, spect = look. With this shift, he was able to use his rational PFC, going from a reflexive irrational limbic response to a reflective rational frontal response. Despite his fear, he went to school the next day, and was greeted cheerfully by the little redheaded girl, who told him how proud she was and that she hoped he would ask her to the tenth-grade social. Jimmy had now moved to another current maximum potential, a new I-M. Jimmy moved from blaming, loathing, and being angry with himself as too weak and scared, to understanding why he was doing what he was doing, and how this was an I-M that he didn't have to like nor condone, but had to respect. He used the Four Rs technique, but it was really shifting the way he saw himself, this small change, that had a big effect.

Jimmy had trusted his imperfect self—the best he could do was fear going to school. That had been his I-M. But rather than blame himself for it, he used the I-M Approach to explore *why* that was the best he could do. Instead of letting irrational fear do what fear is meant to do and make him run from *himself* for not doing the best he could, Jimmy explored how the four domains were interacting and then shifted from his irrational limbic-controlled brain to his rational PFC.

Moving from Reflexive to Reflective

Several critical biological adaptations accelerated our evolutionary success on this planet. For example, our thumbs and being able to stand on two legs instead of four dramatically improved our survival potential. These two adaptations alone gave us an advantage over species that could not grasp things with their hands or weren't able to free up their arms to use those hands more efficiently. Standing up also gave us a slight height advantage: being able to see the tops of the savannah grasses and their movement may have afforded an earlier alert to a predator approaching through those grasses. Our fear reflex is an I-M, a constantly changing current maximum potential in a given moment. It makes no sense from a Darwinian evolutionary perspective that we would evolve anything that was not somehow the best our bodies could do in response to the world around us. Animals that did not do as well did not survive, and that evolutionary line ceased as surely as a child would not survive if born without a functioning brain stem. For most of our evolution, the limbic system has had more control over the majority of our waking moments than our PFC. In practical terms, that car can dart out, the metal bowls may clatter, a door may slam, the brain and body may startle—for what you think affects what you feel. But a quick reactivation of the PFC can assuage the fear so quickly elicited.

If Everyone Is at an I-M, What Happens to the Idea of Being Sick?

In medicine several decades ago, a model of care referred to by the superacademic term the "bio-psycho-social" model was developed by various experts.[11] The idea at that time was to try to integrate our biological world with our worlds of psychology and sociology—all good stuff and done with good intention. But a result of this highly influential way of thinking about medicine is that it has created labels where perhaps none were really needed. Medicine and psychiatry have taken what are actually reasonable responses to the world around us and called people like Jimmy "broken" and "sick."

Much of our inclination to see things as sick stems from our built-in tendency to compare sets of information. Our brain is designed to do just this, as I did when the car suddenly pulled out in front of me, or as Alan did when he heard an unfamiliar sound that turned out to be the family cat. What we have come to call "illness" is really just another manifestation in the myriad of human I-M variations.

We know we feel different when we have a cold than when we don't have a cold. But because our brains have evolved to compare things, we sometimes assume that the difference implies a scale, a "better and worse," "black and white," "illness and wellness," "normal and abnormal." In my field of medicine, things that are "abnormal" have been assigned the term "pathological." Pathology results in an ongoing state of discomfort, which medicine has called a "disease"—literally a dis-easy state of being. Pathology usually results in some sickness that compromises the ability of the person with the sickness to function at his or her "best." Instead, the sick person is at a perceived disadvantage. People who are sick do worse than people who are well. This disadvantage creates a paradigm of "dis-ease," one that can ultimately be traced back to a primordial and limbic fear that you will not survive.

With an infectious disease, we can attribute the difficulty and our body's immune system response to a concrete organism—a bacteria or virus. This invader has penetrated our internal biological domain and influenced our body to respond to the attack. We feel concerned about some people who have contracted a disease. But some people who have an infection like hepatitis or HIV are not treated with such compassion and may be vilified and held responsible for their condition.

We have a similar response to people who have been diagnosed with cancer. Some are treated with compassion; they did not choose to have their own cells rise up in revolt against their own body. But there is disturbing data to support that, if the person has lung cancer and was a smoker, that compassion can instead become a stigma of blame.[12]

Addiction in general is a condition that is still regarded by many as a moral failure or lack of willpower, even though we have long known that the brain chemistry of addicts and alcoholics contributes to their inability to "just say no."

Rather than see that our bodies are responding the best they can to the environment in which they live, we label them as "sick." Asthma, high blood pressure, high cholesterol, diabetes, heart disease, even acne carry with them a subtle stigma. You should be doing better, we say to the overweight person. Or be sure to wash your face more, we say to the kid with acne. These responses serve to alienate these people and make them ashamed and fearful of their imperfection. This way of viewing ourselves and each other has resulted in enormous, if unintended, harm. Why has fear gone so wrong, inhibiting us instead of protecting us? In part, because we have come to believe the idea that if we are not doing the "best" we can by some often arbitrary socially determined criteria, then we must be "sick" and "broken."

A New Way of Thinking about our "Imperfections"

For a long time, our limbic system has been in charge of our brain. From a survival perspective, this has been a remarkably successful strategy for millennia. But just as our proto-hominid ancestors began to outthink their Neanderthal cousins, we can start using the thinking part of our brain to outsmart the feeling part. We can start using our prefrontal cortex, our PFC.

Our growing awareness and consciousness of our PFC *by* our PFC itself suggests an exciting idea. I believe we are on the cusp of another huge leap in our evolutionary process. In this leap, our PFC establishes the logical progression toward its ascendency over our limbic system. One step toward that process is by changing our perspective from a person who's broken or faulty to one who is simply doing the best he or she can at any and every moment in time—seeing ourselves, and everyone, at an I-M. Our limbic system may be afraid of losing its primary control, inducing fear and suggesting retreat from this idea. But when you really think about it, shifting control to the PFC makes a lot of survival sense, and the I-M Approach is a way to get that done. Respect is one of the most powerful forces in our universe.

With the brains we have evolved, we can shift away from viewing ourselves and others as lacking. Where we now see sickness, we can instead appreciate a person, a cell, a behavior, or a country as doing the best they can instead of being inadequate and not doing better. We can begin to use our PFC to see ourselves and each other at an I-M, instead of being sick or broken.

This shift is the foundation and core of the I-M Approach, changing the way we look at each other and ourselves. We now have a more analytical brain that need not lump the world into categories of doing poorly or doing well. When you think about it, it is sort of arrogant to assign that degree of value or non-value onto something—and especially onto someone. I am not convinced that any of us are really in a position to say that someone, including our self, is not doing as well as they should at any given moment. What do we stand to lose by, instead, accepting that they (we) are responding to the world the best they can at this moment? I am suggesting we begin to view each other at an I-M, a current maximum potential.

The I-M Approach reminds us that our biological domain is doing the best it can at each and every moment in time. Just as your body and the cells that comprise that body respond the best they can when you have a cold, I am suggesting we consider each of us as behaving and interacting with the world in the same way: at a current maximum potential, an I-M. I could look at a person who has a cold as sick under the influence of a new environment, one invaded by a virus. Or, I could be amazed by how cool the response to that different influence truly is—the I-M of the biological response of the body, reacting the best it can at this moment in time.

The First Principle of the I-M Approach

A lot changes when we shift to an I-M Approach. Contrast the feeling of being respected and accepted to feeling disrespected and rejected. Consider how differently we respond to people who judge us than to those who accept us. What changes when people begin to view each other as doing the best they can as influenced by the life they have lived? What changes when we begin to view ourselves that way as well? A lot of things change, and I believe for the better. The shift to seeing ourselves and each other at an I-M is a small change with a big effect. Remember that this is the First Principle of the I-M Approach: *small changes have big effects.* If you think you have to change everything, you will be overwhelmed. And feeling overwhelmed leads to feeling afraid. Once you recognize that a small change in any one of the four domains will have a ripple effect throughout the system, you can relax! That shift in perception is appreciated through the second internal domain, the Ic domain of the I-M Approach, which we explore in the next chapter.

2

Rapid Response

The Ic Domain (How "I See" Myself)

"Often, it's not about becoming a new person,
but becoming the person you were meant to be,
and already are, but don't know how to be."
—**Heath L. Buckmaster**, *Box of Hair: A Fairy Tale*

Amanda became a mother at the age of twenty-four. When her daughter was just six months old, Amanda woke up one morning and could not move her left arm. At first she thought she had slept on it wrong. But there was no tingling, no pain, no sensation at all. She just could not move her left arm, which hung limp from her shoulder.

Amanda told me her story while a patient on my ward in the locked in-patient psychiatric unit, after her fear about her paralyzed arm had overwhelmed her. On occasion, she would cradle the arm against her body like a baby, held in place by her right hand grasping her left wrist. If she took away her hand, her left arm would wilt like an unwatered plant, to flop then sway like a pendulum powered only by gravity and not her will.

Everything had been fine just a week before. Her baby was a lovely little girl, and the two had quickly developed a music and rhythm together. When her baby was hungry, Amanda would feed her. When her baby cried, Amanda responded. When her baby slept, Amanda slept. When her baby awoke, Amanda was there to pick her up and comfort her, cradling her in her left arm, safe and snug. Amanda saw herself as a good mother, attentive and caring.

After the child's birth, Amanda's mom would come over often to help her with the baby. Amanda told me how proud her mom had been of her. "You are such a good mother, Amanda," her mom would say. Through the eyes of her own mother, Amanda confirmed her ability as a new mom: a good mother herself, capable and confident.

But on one of the visits, Amanda was holding her baby in her left arm and using her right to reach in the cupboard for a bottle of baby formula when she stumbled. "You'll drop her!" Amanda's mother blurted out. "Careful!" Amanda's mother took the crying baby from Amanda and laid her down, stroking the baby's back to soothe the infant to sleep. Back in the kitchen, Amanda also began to cry, her mother's urgent shout, "You'll drop her!" echoing in her mind.

It was the very next morning that Amanda awoke as usual in response to the soft sound of movement and cooing of her daughter, but found her arm did not respond. Fear took over all of Amanda's senses. How was she going to care for her baby? How was she going to go back to work? Why couldn't she feel her arm? What if she were going to die? One fearful thought led to another. Her desperation grew and she called her mom. Amanda was frozen by fear, afraid she was as useless to her daughter as her arm was to her.

Amanda went from doctor to doctor over the next several days. After several medical examinations, they could find no muscle or bone disease or neurologic disorder. In a panic, she thought she was going crazy and began hyperventilating. She could not be calmed by her mother, who called an ambulance that whisked the frantic twenty-four-year-old woman to an emergency room. There she was evaluated and then sent to the psychiatric hospital where she became my patient.

Fear has an enormous influence on our sense of self, which I call our "Ic domain"—how you see yourself and how you think others see you—and our Ic domain has a huge influence on how we experience fear. Fear prevents most people from trying, taking risks in careers and relationships, expressing themselves fully in life. Fear cripples the self.

Over the next several days, Amanda and I explored her fear. Approaching and confronting one's fear takes enormous courage because the very feeling we are trying to explore is compelling us to run, as it activates our flight response. Yet for all of us, the prize of that exploration holds promise, making it worth the challenge. Amanda thought that she was not a good enough mother, and that her mom was a better mother than she would ever be. How could she protect her daughter? How could she provide for her, feed and clothe her, and change her diapers when she only had one good arm? And if she did ever hold her daughter again, how could she be sure she would not drop her, just as her mother had warned?

Amanda was able to trace the onset of her paralysis to the day before, when her mother's reaction had scared her so. But there was no way, said Amanda, that her arm would become paralyzed just because of that. Her arm remained a flaccid testimony to her incompetence.

The next day, Amanda's mother brought the baby to visit her in the hospital. Her little girl's face blazed with an enormous smile of recognition, and, as her legs began to wiggle in delight, it was the grandmother who nearly lost her grip when the baby pulled away toward the welcoming arms of her mother.

In that moment, Amanda's arms moved—both of them!— fluidly, intuitively, without restriction, toward the little girl who reached for her. She touched her daughter, and the two wrapped in each other's embrace. She was not a bad mom who had to live in fear of dropping her baby, and could once again hold her, confident in her competence as a mother.

Amanda's story may sound bizarre, even unbelievable. But it's true. Amanda had an unusual psychiatric condition called a "conversion disorder," where a strong and often overwhelming emotion is "converted" into a physical response. In this case, Amanda was so afraid she would drop her baby that she shut down any chance of that happening by paralyzing her left arm. Without an arm, she would not even be able to hold her baby, removing any chance of dropping her. That fear exacted an enormous price.

It was no coincidence that her mother's reaction, though unintentional, influenced Amanda to such a high degree. Amanda's mother had influenced her daughter's Ic Domain.

The Ic Domain

Let's look at how my definition of the Ic, or "I See," applies in this case. For the most part, Amanda's mother saw her daughter as a capable mother in her own right. But with that impulsive gasp, "You'll drop her," in an instant, Amanda perceived her mother's view of her change from competent to incapable, perhaps even a threat to her child.

The Ic domain has a tremendous influence over how we experience fear, even to the extent that our minds can affect our bodies, as in Amanda's case. But how does this happen? There is a short answer to this question, known as Theory of Mind, or ToM.

Mind Reading and ToM

Maggie had a piece of candy. She put the candy in a blue box in her kitchen, closed the box, and walked out of the room. A little while later, her mischievous little brother Max went into the kitchen. He saw the blue box and opened it. He knew the candy was Maggie's, but instead of eating it on the spot, he took the candy and put it in a red box, closed both boxes, and left the kitchen. When Maggie comes back into the room, where do you think she will she look for the candy?

I expect that you will say the blue box. That's where Maggie left the candy, that's where Maggie should expect to find the candy. To us, this seems obvious because we have the ability to take Maggie's point of view. That simple yet profound ability is what Theory of Mind is all about: the ability to appreciate someone else's point of view, to take someone else's perspective.

You have a mature and intact Theory of Mind. Most children by the age of four years would also say the blue box, understanding that this is where Maggie would look. But younger children are generally not yet capable of knowing that because they have not developed Theory of Mind. Human beings are not born with ToM, but born with the potential to develop this capacity.

I believe that ToM is the fundamental building block of all human social interaction. Theory of Mind is the natural ability to appreciate and infer what someone else is thinking. But it's not just a fancy psychological theory. We use ToM constantly every day when we're with other people. Have you ever been driving down the road and seen someone drive erratically, switching their blinkers on and off? You probably think to yourself, "What is that person thinking?" Or, when you see someone on the train who has cranked up her MP3 player loud enough to cause everyone to cringe, you're again likely to wonder, "What is that person thinking?" We are always trying to figure out what others are thinking and feeling. And when we sometimes wonder if they're thinking at all, what we are really thinking is, "How could he be so rude as to not notice the way he is making me and everyone else feel!"

This interest and need to understand another human animal has evolved with the development of human social dynamics. It is amazing, when you think about it, how we formed social groups at all. For millions of years, we were mostly solitary, skulking around the jungle or savannah, a small mammal, isolated, alone, and vulnerable. We lived moment to moment, relying on our ancient limbic survival signal, one that compelled us to get away from other animals and retain one's isolation. But in a remarkably short amount of time from an evolutionary perspective, a dramatic change occurred that laid the foundation for humanity as we know it today: humans began to form small social groups.

A solitary individual was always at risk of being eaten by a predator sneaking up from behind, simply because he could only look in one direction at a time. But as soon as you added another set of eyes, another person, that other individual literally could have your back. He watched for predators from a direction that you could not see. This benefit of being close to each other began to outweigh remaining solitary. Assuming that the two of you had some agreement that you would alert the other if a predator appeared, you increased your chance of survival by decreasing your risk of becoming prey. This physical cooperation produced a cognitive analog—the ability to share one's perspective with another person. And more, *the ability to appreciate that another person has a different perception at all.*

Our ancient fear emotions never evolved away, but over time, they have been muted by other emotions and the development of our prefrontal cortex. We began to evolve the ability to ascertain another person's intentions toward us, and then again, what they were hoping for themselves. The survival pressure for this awareness of other humans' minds led us to the development of what we now call Theory of Mind.

This capacity isn't always present at the same level and can vary in effectiveness, depending on our mood, our personality, and the situation. For example, arguing with another person can interfere with our ability to appreciate another person's point of

▶ **ToM AND AUTISM**

Traditionally, scientists have explored ToM through this lens of reciprocal understanding. They have viewed ToM as a form of empathy, an interest in what other people think or feel. But when you look at people on the autistic spectrum, it is the lack of ToM that is the core deficit—a person's difficulty, or basic inability, to appreciate another person's point of view, to know that another person's brain is thinking like theirs is. A person with autism has not developed the proper brain wiring, although the causes of this are unknown.

But autistic people are not the only ones without an intact ToM. Individuals who have suffered trauma to the PFC, have neurodegenerative diseases like Alzheimer's, and even people under the influence of alcohol can exhibit diminished Theory of Mind.[1]

view. How many times has this happened when you are in a fight with a loved one? It should be no surprise, then, that a lack of empathy is associated with very angry and violent people.[2] And many bullies are called "callous children" because they also may have a deficit in ToM. Some bullies have difficulty recognizing that their behaviors cause fear in others. The experience of fear is in response to a perceived threat, so if someone around you does not recognize they scare you, that is a scary person![3]

There is a huge market for scary stories, scary movies, and frightening stories in the news. But there is a line that most societies have drawn between providing scary entertainment and randomly scaring people when it is unexpected. Bullies are considered immoral because they break this basic unspoken rule of our society: don't scare someone or induce fear maliciously. A study out of Georgetown University suggests that many bullies neither recognize the fear they are inducing nor understand that the action is not "morally acceptable."

People who have a deficit in Theory of Mind are often shunned by those who do have an intact ToM. It is disturbing to be around a person who you do not think cares about your feelings or what you think, especially if you sense that person doesn't have the capacity for empathy. Someone like that could be dangerous, so we do not trust them. In other words, a lack of ToM in someone else can activate our limbic system and make us feel afraid. And we, in turn, can make other people afraid of us when we don't use this remarkable part of our PFC.

ToM and the Ic

As we noted, the vast majority of people naturally develop Theory of Mind by the age of four. Imagine a young child and her dad in the garden. The father is cutting some roses and pricks his finger, prompting a yelp. That young child is likely going to come over and ask the dad if he's OK, maybe even go and get a Band-Aid to cover the "boo-boo." That child can appreciate that her dad is hurt, and can, to a degree, appreciate what her father is likely to be thinking and feeling.

We call this interest in another person's thoughts and feelings "empathy." Having empathy for another person is almost universally regarded as an attribute and asset. We gravitate toward people who care about us. Being able to appreciate someone else's point of view is implied in phrases like "good communicator" or "people person." We like to be around people who seem concerned about how we feel. They make us feel good because they appear interested in what we are thinking or feeling. We cannot feel empathy unless we can appreciate what another person's experience and perspective are, and we cannot do this without Theory of Mind.

But I suggest we extend the traditional idea of empathy through ToM even further, beyond being aware of what others are thinking. This is where our Ic comes in: what we are really interested in is *what are you thinking or feeling about me?* This is the real power of this most fundamental part of our humanity. For it is our profound interest in what other people think or feel about us that influences how we begin to view ourselves—and our Ic, how we see ourselves.

From an evolutionary point of view, this makes a lot of sense. A million years ago, as we were evolving as a species, it was much more important from a survival point of view if I thought you were looking at me as your lunch than if I thought you might be hungry. The first is what you are thinking about me. The second is my appreciation of what you are feeling. Once I have assured myself that I am not your lunch, I am more willing to share my food with you to ease your hunger!

When the four-year-old child shows empathy toward her father, she will make her father feel valued and be rewarded by his approval of her behavior. His acknowledgment that she has done something worthy shows her how much he values her for expressing empathy, which in turn will reinforce her empathy. Through the eyes of her father, this little girl is beginning to see herself as valuable. This gives her a feeling of pleasure, a rewarding experience of reciprocity that binds humans together into social groups, families, tribes, and communities.

Theory of Mind (ToM) is a PFC function, the part of our new brain (neocortex) that truly distinguishes us as humans. The PFC communicates this perception to our more ancient limbic brain. The seat of emotions, the limbic system, then tags that perception with an emotion, such as, "Feel good—that person understands what you want and is going to help," or "Feel scared—that person is clueless about what you are feeling." Don't you "know" when a person is listening and seems to care, compared to when they are tuning out? ToM is actively, fluidly, and continuously assessing what another person is thinking or feeling, especially what they are thinking or feeling about you! That's what drives our response, and that's also what can trigger our fear reflex.

Part of the Group

The vast majority of humans do not like being alone for very long. We want to be part of a group. We do not understand people who want to live off the grid and not be around others. We think they must be lonely, and if they are not lonely then there must be something wrong with them. We say things like, "No man is an island." If you've ever seen reality shows like *Survivor* or *The Apprentice*, you'll know that the ultimate punishment was to be voted off the show each week or be "fired." However it happens, elimination from the group means disaster.

And it always has. Our strong evolutionary need to be part of a group, and our intrinsic fear of being an outsider, is what shapes every person's Ic domain. We want to be seen as valuable, for valued people get to stay in the group. Through the eyes of others, we see ourselves as valuable, just like that little girl who gave her dad a Band-Aid. But when we think we are not seen as valuable, we can become very, very afraid.

This is the power of ToM: when I perceive you are thinking about me as a valuable human being, I can relax. I relax because I am not afraid that you or the group might reject me. And not being rejected means I can hang out with you, perhaps even as a friend—or more vitally, be accepted by the significant people in my life. ToM helps create another option to the fight-flight-freeze response: friendship and fellowship. Having a friend increases our sense of value and our own self-esteem. And every friend was once a stranger.

The Power of Our Ic

What are some things that give you a bump in your self-esteem? It's not just when we've accomplished something. It's usually when another person sees and recognizes that we have accomplished something. When we think other people view us with approval, our self-esteem increases. This is one of the reasons we compliment each other on what we wear, how we smell, the kind of car we drive, and how we do on the job.

And when we do get a compliment, it feels great! We get that little rush, that incredible and pleasurable feeling of being seen as valuable when someone else recognizes something positive in us. The Ic domain, influenced by people from our home and social domains, has some effect on the biological domain. That rush is from a very important and relatively new brain chemical, from an evolutionary point of view: oxytocin. When I compliment my kids for an achievement of some sort, or just let them know how special they are, I know what I'm doing to their brain: I'm sending a rush of oxytocin from their brains, which then courses through their bodies. A chemical that originates in the brain but has effects on other parts of the body is called a "neurohormone." Oxytocin is a neurohormone; for example, oxytocin is the neurohormone that tells a mother's uterus to contract when she is about to have her baby.

Oxytocin is called "the cuddle chemical" or "the trust hormone." Just as fear forces the body to release cortisol and epinephrine, the brain releases oxytocin when we feel cared for, appreciated, and valued by another person.[4] In a study out of the University of Sydney, Australia, naturally anxious men who inhaled oxytocin before giving a high-stress speech rated themselves more successful than other men who did not get the pre-speech oxytocin. Oxytocin appears to enhance self-esteem and decreases stress even in people who *don't* have the greatest self-image.[5] On a genetic level, people who had genes that made more oxytocin receptors, implying that oxytocin was more readily accessed and utilized, had more "psychological resources" such as optimism, mastery, and self-esteem, compared to people who had genes that made fewer oxytocin receptors.[6]

In fact, how you feel about yourself has a physiological effect not just in your mind, but on your actual brain. Scientists in Austria used MRIs to measure brain sizes of forty-eight healthy adults. They also gave them tests that measured self-esteem. It turns out that the subjects who had higher levels of self-esteem also had a larger prefrontal cortex than those with less self-esteem.[7]

Self-esteem's impact on the brain is something we should all keep in mind, especially when raising children. Our interest in what other people think or feel about us has protective importance as well. Perhaps the most compelling research on the protective nature of being seen as valuable by others comes from studies of resilient children. There are some kids who go through the most terrible abuse and neglect who still seem to do well in life, scarred perhaps by what happened to them, but not carrying the open wounds of their trauma. These resilient children have had at least one person in their lives who saw them as valuable. How cool is that? Being seen as valuable, "talented," is a protective factor against the horrendous experiences in their lives, contributing to another powerful factor in resilience: self-esteem.[8]

Our interest in being social has been reinforced over millennia through the interaction of these two powerful modalities—our PFC and the emergence of Theory of Mind—and the pleasure we get from being social and trusting another human being, reinforced by the chemical of trust, oxytocin.

The Ic domain is the entry point of our perception of the world around us—our home and social domains. ToM is a powerful way to feel safe and valuable. The I-M capitalizes on this fundamental part of human nature as a position of respect. Respect leads to value and value leads to trust. But unfortunately, since we human beings are indeed so interested in what other people think or feel about us, ToM has a dark side: it can make us feel *dis*respected and *de*valued, lead to *mis*trust, and result in fear.

▶ NARCISSISM VERSUS FEAR OF REJECTION

People have always loved filling in those questionnaires—whether they be numerology, personality, intelligence, or career quizzes—that tell them what they were truly meant to do with their lives and what secret desirable qualities they hold. In the past, you might have found these in newspapers and magazines. But today, the same types of quizzes are rife on the Web. They're used in advertising, as chain mail, and on Facebook and other social media. The key difference in the social media age is that the results are not designed to be private anymore.

"People have always been taking quizzes like this," said futurist Sherry Turkle in a recent *Wired* magazine article. "But [before social media], you were doing it for yourself." Today, she notes, these quizzes are designed for performance. "Here, part of the point is to share it, to feel 'who you are' by how you share who you are. [It's] the conflation of *who you are* and *who thinks you're okay*." The focus on declaring who you are rather than just *being* is "a nonstop, exhausting performance," says Turkle, who believes, along with other social theorists, that this is all something new to our evolution as individuals and as a society.

While the majority of these quizzes are really just pointless diversions that tell us little about our true selves, it's important to look at how we use these and other new social media tools to promote our social selves. The narcissists may be better at doing this than others, but we all are doing it for essentially the same reason—to be valued and accepted.[9]

Undermining Fears—Changing an I-M

Billy was an overweight and clumsy third grader who didn't have a lot of friends and lacked self-confidence. He was the kid who was always on the outskirts of the playground, not in the middle of the play. But his teacher made him the pencil sharpener monitor, and he would sharpen the pencils for her and give them to the rest of the class. This was a big deal in third grade, and he would solemnly take the pencils and deliver them from desk to desk. Some of the kids said thank you. The next day more of the kids said thank you, and by the third day, Billy was having mini-conversations with every kid in the room. By the end of the week, Billy was initiating the conversation. "Here's your pencil, Frances." "Thanks Billy," chirped Frances.

As his self-esteem improved, the teacher created a new class position of "Pencil Sharpener of the Week." Billy ceremoniously taught the next PSW (as the class had named it) the best way to use the pencil sharpener, graciously stepped down, and another kid took his place. By the end of the school year, every kid had been the PSW. By then Billy felt part of the group, in the classroom and on the playground.

Billy was not asked to "prove himself" by his teacher. She intuitively knew he was at an I-M in which he did not trust himself to be successful. So the teacher did it for him—she trusted that he could do the job of a PSW. When Billy, and the rest of the classroom, recognized (a PFC function) that the teacher trusted him, it secured his position in the group, he felt calmer (a limbic function), and the threat of being alone subsided. His teacher respected him, valued him, and had trust in him. Her confidence became Billy's confidence.

Billy's self-esteem was a function of comparison: Am I as cool as that kid, as rich as that kid, as smart as that kid, as attractive as that kid? That's just the way our brains work, always comparing sets of information. How we interpret that information is more under our control than we recognize. Billy's perception of himself must have included some comparison, either between himself and other people, or between himself as he is and the future Billy he wanted to be but did not believe he could attain. When the teacher drew attention to him with a position of honor in the group, that self-image shifted. His teacher saw him as valuable, so perhaps he was indeed valuable, which reduced his fear of failure in the classroom and on the playground. As his Ic changed, his I-M improved and his fears subsided.

Fear has to have a place of fertile ground to flourish. The seed of fear finds such a place in our deep human desire to be valued by another human being. But in order to feel valued or devalued, one first has to be able to appreciate that another person has a perspective of the world from their own point of view: Theory of Mind (ToM).

In this story, Billy's teacher was acutely aware of his struggles. As an experienced teacher, she also knew she could change how the other kids viewed him, and in the process changed how he viewed himself. As a result, Billy's I-M changed, and in fact, so did everyone else's.

Different Views of the Same Thing

Try this: Look straight ahead and close your left eye. Now look straight ahead but close your right eye. Notice how your perspective changes just a little bit because of the slightly different positions of your eyes?

Think about this: Each of us has to have a slightly different visual perspective of the world because we can never occupy exactly the same place in the world. Multiply that by seven billion people, each one with a unique set of experiences, and you have an amazing challenge. What do they think of you? And each person, whether they want to admit it or not, has a concern about what you think of him. This is the potential breeding ground for fear, especially if there is not the foundation of trust already in place. And it is exactly this fear that can influence each of us to freeze in our tracks, worried that we will be judged as inadequate by another person. The Ic domain, through ToM, is the entry point of our surrounding world into our image of ourselves.

The stories of all the people in this book, along with the vast majority of us in the world, have been influenced by what we perceive other people think and feel about us since at least the age of four years old, and perhaps younger. This ancient survival-based interest is a double-edged sword: when we see ourselves as valuable through the eyes of another, we begin to trust. But if we see that other people view us as inadequate, we can begin to fear. This is the side of Theory of Mind that can make us fear.

Fear decreases our ability to appreciate what another person is really thinking or feeling, decreasing empathy, and likely increasing a similar experience in the other person, or making them angry instead, which would only increase our own fear. This critical piece of information has enormous utility next time you become afraid. It is critical to keep the prefrontal cortex (PFC)—the seat of critical thinking, the ability to interpret information— working, as your brain will try to revert to a limbic survival mode, and your choices will be reduced to fight, flight, or freeze.

But there is a fourth option—that of fellowship, which is a function of trust. In the limbic survival mode, however, trust may feel more elusive, as you will have shut down any ability to truly understand what that other person is indeed thinking or feeling, which will then have an influence on his or her Ic domain. In this way, fear breeds fear.

Chances are pretty good that if you're reading this book, you are someone who has an intact Theory of Mind. Given that you know how to interpret signals from others and feel empathy, to whom have you expressed a sense of value? And how did you show this? Did you need to tell the other person, or did you show this in another way? What about another person's expression of how they value you? How do you know you can trust some of your colleagues? Friends? And how do you know when you cannot?

Even though we may not realize it, we use Theory of Mind all the time. We are fluidly assessing, as part of our natural selection, what other people are thinking or feeling about us. We may not always be aware of the influence we have on each other, innocently inducing fear or trust in another person as effortlessly and thoughtlessly as breathing—just as Amanda's mother did in her reaction to Amanda's juggling of her baby. And yet, if we were indeed to think about the implications of shifting from an impulsive limbic brain (fear) to a more controlled and thoughtful one (trust), my guess is that each of us would rather have someone trust than fear us, just as we would rather trust than fear. Trust brings with it the promise of an alliance. Fear brings with it the potential of that person retreating and leaving us alone and vulnerable, or retaliating with anger, with the intention of making us afraid. The first, the promise of alliance, is much more pleasurable. If the brain is going to choose between fear and pleasure, it will choose pleasure every time. It really is better to have someone's back, and for them to have yours.

Using Our PFC

So what's the big deal about being afraid anyway? It's been great for survival for millions of years. And yet, we all intuitively know that fear itself has a downside. In a state of fear, our thinking brain begins to shut down. A study out of Germany took thirty healthy women and showed them threatening or scary pictures, along with neutral pictures, and measured how much their eyes were blinking. The more eye-blinking, the greater those pictures were thought to stimulate fear in the observing women.

Then the women were given a brain scan while doing another exercise called the "Taylor Aggression Paradigm" (TAP). TAP is an exercise in which a person can give an electric shock to a fictitious opponent. The intensity of that shock is actually measuring the aggression level of the study subject. Women who demonstrated more fearful responses were just as likely to give shocks as those women who were not as fearful. But the more fearful women had more significant decreases in activity of their PFC, or less ability to use that part of their brain responsible for ToM, and were more likely to administer more intense shocks. Being afraid decreases our ability to appreciate what someone else is thinking or feeling, and decreases our ability to reflect on ourselves.[10] Once again, if I am afraid that you may be looking at me as your lunch, I am not really going to care if you are hungry—just that you don't eat me! It will be easier to inflict harm on you if I do not care as much about how you will feel. When scared women administered the electric shock in this study, they simultaneously muted their ability to use ToM, meaning they shut down empathy.

Reading Really Is Fundamental

As ToM is so influential in establishing relationships, how do we exercise this important component of who we are? Interestingly enough, at least one study shows that one way to exercise ToM is to read literary fiction! Researchers from the New School for Social Research in New York found that adults who mainly read works of fiction were more adept at predicting what another person thought or felt, in comparison to adults who mainly read works of nonfiction.[11] This may have enormous impact for our schools, for how we spend our leisure time, and for whether you should be reading this book or one that just has a bunch of stories about my patients! But what this research really implies is that our ability to use ToM can be taught, enhanced, and fine-tuned. Our Ic domain is as fluid as anything else, and ToM is a tool that can be honed with practice into an amazing and easy way to help someone else be less fearful.

▶ LOOK AGAIN AT LOOKS

You can't judge a book by its cover, but boy oh boy, do we ever do this a lot, especially when it comes to people. In a study out of the University of Texas, Austin, forty-six adults and forty-two children were asked to rate virtual-world avatars based on how attractive they were. Both adults and children were then given an option of playing with any of the avatars. The majority of people of both age groups played more with the attractive avatars than the less attractive ones. Even in a video game, our brains are drawn toward physically attractive people.[12] In a world where people of all ages are indeed quick to judge a book by its cover, it's no wonder so many people become concerned with how other people think they look. When you go to a job interview, you don't wear your pajamas. When you go to a sports event, if you wear the colors and logo of the visiting team, expect to be treated differently than if you show up with the home team's insignia. When you are trying to meet a potential partner for the first time, unfortunately or not, how you look is going to influence your access to that person. Not until later do we begin to assess what is actually inside that book. This small and subtle fear can blossom into full-blown social phobia, a fear of being among people for reasons that are not readily conscious but have profoundly activated the limbic flight response. Our entire being can become paralyzed, just like Amanda's left arm.

Fear Starts Young

Infants between the ages of eight and fourteen months begin to experience separation anxiety, a feeling of distress when they are removed from a caregiver. The process itself involves several developmental foundations, which include an understanding that things have some permanence and do not just disappear, a memory of a caregiver, and an ability to recognize the difference between a familiar face and that of a stranger. Put together that the person to whom they have become attached and whom they rely on for nurturing has gone with the presence of a potential predator, and the infant experiences fear, often protesting loudly to alert the missing caregiver of the potential danger. Children that age may not have a word for fear, but they experience it nonetheless.

But at what age does a child begin to recognize that someone else is experiencing fear? Scientists from Boston College in Massachusetts found that even three-year-olds are adept at recognizing the fearful face and body posture of a scared person. But when presented with just the voice of a fearful person, kids were nowhere near as good as they were at recognizing a sad voice.[13]

Because ToM is in place so early in our development, children are just as interested in what other people think about them as adults are. As such, little kids can experience just as much fear. When you get right down to it, our fear is based not just on a fear of death, but a fear of rejection. That is why being seen as valuable is extremely important. As long as we are of value to someone else, we secure our place in the protective group.

This interest in other people's evaluation of us starts very young. In a study out of the Netherlands, 188 children ages ten to thirteen played a computer game that was rigged to give them either positive or negative feedback. Children who already had more social anxiety had a much greater increase in self-esteem when given positive feedback, compared to same-age kids who did not have social anxiety. But those same kids also had great decreases in their self-esteem when given negative feedback.[14] This exquisite sensitivity to the opinion of others is a function of our Ic domain and Theory of Mind.

Labels and Comparing

Earlier I wrote about the term "pathology" in relation to medical illness and talked about how this labeling of "illness" is no longer confined to disorders of our body: the idea of sickness has spread to the world of behaviors. We throw around diagnostic labels like "depression," "schizophrenia," "anxiety," and "addiction," at times without truly appreciating the impact it may have on the person who often has to "carry" the diagnosis like a yoke. To underline the deviation of these behaviors, we add the word "disorder," as in "anxiety disorder," "depressive disorder," "attention deficit disorder," and others. We have ignored the influence of ToM and our desire to help by giving behaviors a name; we may have contributed to the very "sickness" we are trying to cure.

Because of our need to define what's "normal" and "abnormal" by assigning labels, we call these psychiatric conditions "diseases" and can muster at least a modicum of compassion and pity for the person who suffers from the illness. We may not trust them if we perceive their behavior as, by definition, "irrational," but we can pity them.

But very often we still consider unproductive or difficult behaviors as the result not of a disease, but of a moral failing or weakness of will. A depressed person should "snap out of it." An addicted person should "just say no." But for the most part, our human compunction to compare lumps people into groups of those who are "productive" versus those who are "lazy"; those who are "good" and those who are "bad"; those who are "strong" and those who are "weak"; those who are "cowardly" and those who are "brave."

Human beings are very, very skilled at seeing the worst in each other, not to mention fearing each other. We can be astonishingly cruel to those who most need our help, including people with psychiatric conditions or addiction, people in poverty, or those who do not share our belief system. We often turn our backs, using the excuse that the person is somehow not trying hard enough or is somehow inherently flawed, so why should we spend our time helping them? More than just communicating fear to them, we sometimes project disgust. And if that isn't enough, there are times when we see another person helping a person we have rejected and we try to protect ourselves from guilt by using labels like "enabling," so we feel justified in looking down on both "enabler" and "enabled." We are often quick to judge and are also quick to get angry when judged ourselves from beyond the confines of our protective group.

The I-M Approach can change all of that. As a psychiatrist, I have been impressed with the resilience of our human nature, but also its fragility and susceptibility to our ancient emotions. Fear has been part of our evolution, an emotion that can have an impact in an instant that lasts a lifetime. Without fear we would never have survived the potential threats of predators or marauding bands of territorial competitors. Without fear we would never have evolved morals and ethics, the substrate of religion, and the foundation of law. Fear has had a pivotal role in our development as a species, but it has also become a source of incapacitating terror, threatening to rob us of our ability to explore the world, experience joy, and reach out to each other for companionship, protection, and cooperation—just as if our arm were as paralyzed as Amanda's.

The Second Principle of the I-M Approach

The Ic domain, grounded in Theory of Mind, can manifest in the blink of an eye—with a word, a look, an inflection of the voice, a shrug of the shoulder, the wave of a hand, or the shake of a fist, our brains can attribute intention to other people. We theorize about their thoughts and feelings instantly. In fact, these first impressions are formed extremely quickly, within the first thirty-nine milliseconds.[15] There are 1,000 milliseconds in a second. Now that is truly a rapid response.

At any given time, everyone has an I-M. You are part of someone's home or social domain and have an influence on his or her

Ic and biological domains. This leads to the second principle of the I-M Approach: *You control no one but influence everyone.* Think about this for a moment: you have an influence on every single person with whom you come in contact. Everyone. You get to choose the influence you want to be. Now that is power, and an enormous responsibility.

In his terrific book *The Company of Strangers,*[16] Paul Seabright talks about the day he went into a store and bought a shirt made of cotton and how it occurred to him that years ago a complete stranger had to plant the seeds to grow that cotton. Other strangers cultivated it, harvested it with machines built by other strangers, and other strangers drove it in trucks built by yet other strangers to a factory run by more strangers, who dyed it and wove it into a shirt. Other strangers then drove it to a store run by strangers, who put it on a rack so any one of us could walk in and buy it, perhaps even with a credit card, which basically is saying, "Let me take this from you today and I promise you'll be paid for it later." It is mind-blowing! All these people we will never meet have had an influence on the very clothes we're wearing, and when we bought that shirt or skirt or pair of pants, we then had an influence on all those people that we will never meet. We truly do control no one but influence everyone.

Imagine for a moment how the Ic domain is influenced by the I-M Approach. Your brain will respond one way if I see you as doing the best you can at every moment, at an I-M, and differently if I see you as not doing as well as I think you should. This is the power of respect, and the devastating power of feeling inadequate. The biological and Ic domains do not happen in a vacuum. They are in response to two external domains, the first of which is home, which we'll explore in the next chapter.

3

Unexpected Undercurrents

The Home Domain

"What the mind doesn't understand, it worships or fears."
—**Alice Walker**

Sandra lay awake in her bed imagining an oven big enough to cook children and turn them into gingerbread. She imagined meeting a stranger in the woods, a big wolf dressed in clothes who had a really friendly smile but who she knew was trying to take her away from her home. A thought of a delicious-looking apple popped into her head, but perhaps it was poisoned. How was she meant to know? Earlier that night she had eaten an apple, then watched the Disney cartoon *Snow White*. Her breathing quickened and she went to find a parent. But her dad just shook his head, and she thought he may have even laughed a bit. He told her to toughen up, that it was silly to think that someone would poison her apple. But her mom had looked worried.

The next day Sandra felt sick in school and went to the nurse's office, for the third time that week. The nurse called Sandra's mom, who came and picked her up, but instead of driving home, they went to the pediatrician's office for a checkup. There must be something wrong with you, her mom had said. Sandra felt her heartbeat increase, and she felt even sicker to her stomach. There must be something wrong, or why would she be going to the doctor?

Sandra sat across from me in my office, now thirty-three years old, unmarried, underemployed, sure that she should not bother going to the job interview she had the next day for a position that had opened up in her firm. "Why should they hire me?" She had not shown up for a blind date her friends had set up for her the night before. Why should she, the guy wasn't going to like her anyway. She was just not pretty enough, not smart enough, not good enough. Not strong enough. Sandra had all sorts of physical symptoms: headaches, stomachaches, a general sense of "dis-ease." She had three dead bolts on the front door of her apartment. She was like a little girl who could be snatched away at any time, just like those girls she had heard about when her dad had read her fairy tales before bed. Sandra was able to laugh a little. "Here you go, sweetie. Here's a story about a witch who lures kids into her home with a sweet smile then tries to cook them in an oven. Sweet dreams! Night! Love you!" She avoids apples to this day.

The home domain of the I-M is powerful. No one is going to deny that the home we grow up in has an enormous influence on who we are today. Think back for a moment on your own home, and how it has influenced the decisions you have made in the rest of your life. Was your mom afraid of spiders and are you? How about snakes? Dentists?

When your parents cautioned you to look both ways before you crossed the street, I am sure you did. But how cautious are you today? How did you take that familiar phrase, "Curiosity killed the cat" or "Don't swim until an hour after you eat"? And when they said, "Don't talk to strangers," did that have an influence on how comfortable you feel going up to a stranger at a party and

starting a conversation? Amazing isn't it, how these early, innocent experiences may continue to have influence all these years
later. Innocuous as these warnings may be, they can also have a
deep and long-lasting effect on what you fear, and how much.

The Home Domain Is Not a Blame Game

Before I go any further in this chapter on the home domain, let
me be crystal clear that this is not about blaming parents. Years
ago, it was popular to fault parents for how bad their kids were
doing. Theories like "The Refrigerator Mother" suggested that
cold and aloof parents were responsible for inducing schizophrenia
and autism in their children. There is no question that the home
in which we have grown up has had an enormous influence on
our I-M. This is not to excuse any behaviors of any of us, child or
parent, but rather to respect them using the I-M Approach.

Blame has never done any good. Blame creates a barrier to
truly exploring why we do what we do. That barrier is based on
our imagination and fear that we will be viewed as lacking, bad,
inadequate, and therefore at risk of being kicked out of our protective group because we have no value. There is ample evidence
that people who think they are going to be blamed or judged negatively are less likely to seek help or dare looking at themselves
honestly. They don't trust anyone, especially themselves.

I am not trying to blame anyone. I am not a judge, but a psychiatrist, interested in why people do what they do. Parents are
also at their I-M, given the influence of their interaction with the
four domains, including their home domain and parents, who
were at their I-M. When those behaviors are viewed as an I-M, we
can explore them without moral overlay and judgment, just wondering why a person is doing what he or she is doing.

I hope to instill the same wonder in you.

So, I encourage both parents and their children to keep reading! One of the audience participation things I do in my lectures

is to ask audience members who are parents to raise their hands. Many do. Then I ask, "Could anyone who has had parents please raise their hands?" and of course people laugh, and then everyone raises their hands. We have all had parents. And all of them have been at their I-M.

Blame and responsibility are two different things. When each of us takes responsibility for our I-M, truly amazing things can happen. Relax. You are doing the best you can. With this in mind, let's explore, however, how our home domain may have subtly, or not so subtly, influenced the fear reflex we have as adults.

The Acquisition of Fear

How do human beings acquire fear at all? In the last chapter, we discussed the conditioned response, something learned by an animal when exposed to an event, a stimulus that caused the cortisol response of our biological domain. But in 1977, a scientist in England, Stanley Rachman, noted that some people are scared of things they have never encountered.[1]

Rachman suggested that people can also develop fear vicariously, listening to fear experienced by another person. He did not know about mirror neurons, but we do. It makes intuitive sense that a scary story would result in, well, a scared person. We now know that just watching a scared face can activate mirror neurons in our own brain.[2] When we see a person telling a story and making a scared face, our brains start thinking: Should I be scared as well?

Drilling Down on Fear

Let's take dentists as a great example of vicarious fear. There are several reasons people develop fear of dentists. Some are based on past traumatic experiences, but many are due to the influence of other people and the media.[3] Movie images provide some of the most vivid examples of torture and teeth going hand in hand, like in *Marathon Man,* or the sadistic caricature of dentists portrayed by Steve Martin in the musical comedy *The Little Shop of Horrors.* But these particular reasons cannot be applied to children.

Early on in kids' lives, they will need to start going to the dentist to learn how to properly care for their teeth, so it's counterintuitive for kids to become afraid of a caregiver. Yet they do. So how do kids become afraid of dentists?

Tory was one of my ten-year-old patients who would break into a cold sweat just thinking about the dentist. It may have been the way Tory's older brother raised his eyebrows, or the way Tory's dad lowered his voice as he said the word "dentist," but by the age of seven, the poor child was terrified of the annual dental checkup. There might be drillings, fillings, and pain awaiting in that big chair. The nail in the coffin for Tory was when she overheard her mom whispering to the dentist, "Can I come in and hold her hand?"

In my field we call the erroneous belief that something bad is going to happen, even before experiencing the event, "cognitive vulnerability." Tory's parents had cognitive vulnerability of their own about going to the dentist. They are not alone. Recently, researchers at the University of Madrid interviewed nearly 300 parents and 185 of their kids, looking at how fear of the dentist might be transmitted to kids—the kids' fears directly connected to their parents' fears. Parents with more cognitive vulnerability, this study showed, transmitted distorted thinking to their kids about the horrible things that happen at the dentist's office.[4] But this is something most parents are doing without even being aware of it. All you have to do is spend a little time looking at YouTube.

Some parents videotape their kids in the throes of getting their ears pierced, their hair cut, or getting shots. The running commentaries of these videos could scare anyone. While I am not sure why anyone would want to film their child during a moment of fear or suffering, YouTube is filled with videos of children, in anguish, and in the "clutches" of the dentist. Scientists from the University of Hong Kong in China selected and transcribed twenty-seven YouTube videos of thirty-two different children at the dentist. The kids were crying, screaming, and shivering. They expressed worry, panic, helplessness, and insecurity. In later interviews, the researchers found many kids had developed this fear from the influence of parents.[5]

"Children's fear can be instilled by careless words from parents. A video depicted the destructive behaviors of a young girl who refused to be examined in the clinic. After tiring persuasion and struggle, her mother explained to the dentist that she was acting uncooperatively and irrationally because her father had told her in a teasing tone that, 'the dentist would pull your teeth.'"[6]

As a psychiatrist, I am quite sure that my business will thrive as a result of all of this particular I-M of parenting!

But the end result of all of this fearmongering (mostly unintentional, one hopes) is sometimes not just fear itself. Scientists from Brazil took information from the Children's National Immunization Campaign in Pelotas, Brazil, and studied 608 mothers to explore the effect on a child of the mother's anxiety about dentists. They found that the mothers who were anxious themselves about the dentist not only communicated that anxiety to their kids, but seemed less likely to take their kids to the dentist at all. The result: those kids had more cavities![7]

Let's examine this particular fear through the lens of the I-M Approach.

The I-M and the Dentist

We can use the I-M Approach to decrease this fear, and others, in yourself and thereby your children (if you have any), and reset your fear reflex in the home domain. As you'll recall from the last chapter, through the Ic domain we control no one but influence everyone. Children are profoundly influenced and interested in what their parents think or feel, and through their parents' subtle behaviors, they pick up the fear that a dental visit causes their parents. The limbic system in the biological domain activates when a small change is perceived, such as a whisper, a look in the eye, a sweaty palm.

Remember, a small change can have a big effect. An unintended careless word by a parent may trigger a tiny terror response. A phrase intended to calm, such as "it doesn't hurt too much," can, in a certain context, evoke near panic! Even though the child may have never been to the dentist, he or she begins to associate that particular social domain as one of pain and danger. This idea gets logged in the memory part of the limbic system, ready to be activated by the tiny terror of going to get your teeth checked. This small change has had a big effect, the best response this child's Ic and biological domains could achieve.

Parents using the I-M Approach can more readily accept their own fear of dentists. They can use the Four Rs of the cognitive-behavioral therapy technique that we learned in chapter one—recognize, rate, remember, reflect—and become reflective rather than reflexive. First recognize the fear, rate it from 1 to 10, remember that your fear is like a wave and will diminish, and then reflect, by which you remember where your fear of dentists originated and evaluate that memory's relevance to the current situation. Your growing calm is mirrored as you achieve a different I-M for yourself and your child. Another powerful approach is to engage the dentist, and honestly, without embarrassment because it is an I-M, tell her of your fear. When the dentist can respond to a patient's fear directly and instill trust, that patient has an easier experience in the dentist's office.[8] And when you combine these interventions with the road map to insight from the I-M Approach, you emerge with a deeper understanding of why a fear of dentists is your particular I-M. Knowledge and understanding are power, and power is a great tool to combat fear.

▶ **NO FINGER-POINTING ALLOWED**

As much as the influence of parents' fears affects their children, it's important to understand that parents are not to "blame." This is worth repeating. The focus here is on how tremendously, but unconsciously, influential we are in another person's I-M, especially when it comes to the home domain and its impact on developing minds. In my optimistic view of humanity, I am convinced that most parents, anxious or not, when enlightened and instructed, would assess what they tell their kids in an effort to prevent creating anxious kids.

Fear is not comfortable, and the vast majority of parents want nothing more than to ward off discomfort from their children. The I-M of an anxious parent, or any parent, is not to be anything but respected. But that doesn't mean that parents can't accept their anxiety and then do something to change. Even a small change can have a big influence on the I-M of their children and loved ones within the home domain.

The dentist is just one of the many fears that are unwittingly introduced and instilled in the home domain. There are many others, like a fear of snakes or spiders or swimming in the ocean. But let's look at how critical the influence of the home domain remains—perhaps the most influential in the developing brain and Ic domain of every individual.

Attachment and the Home Domain

Many years ago, Dr. John Bowlby, a British psychiatrist, asked a simple but provocative question: Why do parents care for their children? For the rest of his career, this question was the focus of his work, as he developed his Theory of Attachment. Bowlby, Mary Ainsworth, and others eventually identified five types of attachment between a parent and child: secure, anxious, avoid-ant, ambivalent, and disorganized.[9] All of them have an influence through the Ic domain, which results in a response by the biologi-cal domain.

Secure Attachment

Have you ever been to a playground and watched the kids and their caregivers? Some kids are checking things out, and every now and then one heads back to Mom or Dad. When the child gets there, the parent stops whatever he or she may be doing; maybe gives the kid a hug but definitely acknowledges the re-turn; takes the time to stop, look, and listen; and then waves as the kid sets off to explore again. If the kid has come back to the parent crying with a scraped knee or some distress, the parent comforts the kid; stops, looks, and listens; calms the kid down; and comforts him until he is ready to go off and explore the play-ground again. In my office, the child of such a parent may protest a little when the parent leaves, and gives a hug when the parent returns, usually sharing the picture he has drawn or the game he has been playing. These kids have no doubt that their parents see them as valuable and capable. This is a secure attachment.

Anxious Attachment

Some kids at the playground don't venture very far from their parents, clinging to them even as they may wistfully watch the other kids at play. I see a lot of these kids in my practice, glued to their parent's lap instead of playing with the colorful and inviting toys in my office. These kids cry and protest if their parents try to leave the office, clinging to their parent and refusing to sepa-rate. The parent is also too protective, not letting the kid take any risks, making the child more dependent and less independent. If a kid begins to cry, these parents are all over it, being overly comforting to the point where a small boo-boo can seem like a life-threatening wound. I had a mother who was so nervous about her five-year-old boy getting hurt that she would not let him make paper swords in my office, *paper* swords. These kids absorb this message through their Ic domain, leading them to believe their parents love them but see them as incapable, vulnerable, and unable to fend for themselves. This is an anxious attachment.

Avoidant Attachment

Ever see a kid scrape his knee on the playground and run crying to his parent to get some comfort, only to have the grown-up show very little response, instead telling the kid to "get over it," or "be a man"? When this happens enough, that kid's brain becomes conditioned, and he does not expect any real compassion from his parent. No surprise that a kid like this in my office doesn't seem to care if the parent is in the room or not, and doesn't even bother going over to the parent when she does return. These kids are just as likely to treat a stranger the same way as their parent. Children like this may feel as if they have no value through the Ic domain. Their self-esteem erodes, and some seem angry and oppositional. These kids are shutting down ToM: Why would they want to know what someone else is thinking or feeling when the message is no one cares about them because, in their minds, they are not important or valuable? Shutting down ToM can make these kids oblivious to their influence on another person's I-M: the result can be a child who is at extremely high risk of a lifetime of disrupted and unsatisfying relationships. This is an avoidant attachment.

Ambivalent Attachment

Some kids do not know what to expect when they scrape their knee and go to their parent for comfort. One time the parent may be comforting as in a secure attachment, at others dismissive as in an avoidant attachment. This unpredictability results in kids who are not sure what to think of their parents: Can I trust them to comfort me or not? Or how the parents see them: Do they see me as valuable or not? A child like this in my office will protest loudly and vigorously when the parent leaves and remain upset in her absence, but does *not* seek her out when the parent returns to the room. Instead, the child may snub the parent, as if she matters no more to him than he feels he matters to the parent. These kids are always on edge, always fearful, as they cannot trust that other people, especially their parents, have their back. This is called an "ambivalent attachment."

Disorganized Attachment

Some kids on the playground remain on the outskirts of the play, not engaging with other kids. If they do scrape their knee, they may walk backward toward their parent for a hug, bumping into their parent repeatedly, trying to get their parent to raise and wrap her arms around them in an embrace. This type of attachment described by Bowlby is really bizarre, and takes ambivalent attachment to an entirely different level. Some of these kids in my office can appear almost autistic or even completely out of touch with reality, which in my field we call "psychotic." I knew one kid who rocked back and forth, standing in a corner of the room. He looked autistic but wasn't. Instead he seemed terrified of the world around him, unsure and uncertain what to expect. Another would only meet with me in the waiting room, too frozen and fearful to even come into the office. The parents of this kid did not try to soothe their child. Instead, the parents came off as pretty scary. One of them actually forcibly picked up the kid and carried him into my office. That child did not protest, but did not move from where his parent placed him, instead beginning to rock and look anywhere but at my face. All too often this type of relationship is suggestive of abuse and maltreatment of the child. These kids have never felt valued. Instead their existence is one in which they believe they are so worthless they do not deserve to be respected. These kids have enormous difficulty connecting to anyone, and basically have shut themselves down from the world. Why should they want to know what anyone thinks or feels about them if it is always malevolent? This type of attachment is appropriately called "disorganized."

Some parents reading this may worry that they're not providing the right kind of attachment. Have no fear. Kids bring their own way of responding to the world to these relationships and parent-child attachments. One of my sons was really anxious about starting kindergarten. This doesn't mean he had an anxious attachment. He was just worried about the change from his home to social domain. When he and I went to the first day of school, he at first sat snug on my lap. But then he and I were able to joke a bit, laugh a bit, and he began to move away from me and explore, even though I remained in the room. On occasion, he would come back and check to see if I were still there, and I was. But on the second day, he was fine with me staying for a few minutes, then leaving. He waved good-bye to me from across the room, happily engaged with some new friends. Even though he appeared anxious at first, he did not have an anxious attachment.

——————— Exercise ———————

HOW ATTACHED ARE YOU?

I'd like you to give some thought to the attachment style of your parents, and if you are a parent, your own style of parenting. This is important because the I-M Approach suggests that all of these forms of attachment are the best a parent and child can do given the influence of the four domains. But if we view one as better than another then we are not really applying the I-M Approach. The I-M Approach is without judgment. While reading about the child coming to share something with a receptive parent, you probably felt different than when reading about the parent who ignored, dismissed, or forcibly picked up the child. Now, I am asking you to try to understand these different attachment styles through an I-M lens. You don't have to like it or condone it, but wondering why the attachment is the way it is will yield far greater results than dismissing the forms as just "bad" parenting. So, in that spirit, which one are you, which one are your parents, and how did the four domains influence this particular I-M? If upon reflection you uncover that yours was an insecure or anxious attachment, how do you think this may be contributing, even now, to the fears you experience, the confidence you may lack, and the barriers you perceive to feeling and being "more" successful, or a different I-M?

The Influence of the Home Domain on the Ic

Why is this attachment in childhood so important anyway? And how does it impact our capacity for developing and handling fear throughout our lives? After all, we are not kids anymore. One would think we might outgrow early familial influences over time. But the type of attachment you grew up with in your home domain has an enormous influence on the type of attachment you are more likely to create as an adult. And this can have its own consequences, especially when it comes to fear.

Even though it is common sense that the type of relationship you had growing up with your parents is going to have an impact on your I-M as an adult, it is worth noting that this is supported by many studies, including a large one out of Queens College in Flushing, New York. Researchers reviewed data from 8,098 people ages fifteen to fifty-four. Relationships with parents influenced how happy and secure people were, and how well they were doing as adults at work and in their own relationships. People who reported poor-quality relationships with their parents reported as adults more depression and fear, avoidant and dependent relationships of their own, and poorer social functioning in general.[10]

The Biological Domain as a Measure of Attachment

The four domains that influence a person's I-M—biological, Ic, home, and social—are intimately connected. So it should be no surprise that these attachment patterns are reflected in a child's response to stress or fear. We can actually quantify these responses by measuring levels of the stress hormone, cortisol. That's what researchers from Portugal did when they assessed the quality of attachment between fifty-one children, ranging in age from eighteen to twenty-six months, and their mothers. In their study, published in the journal *Developmental Psychobiology*, they found that when a secure child was challenged with a scary event, his cortisol levels went up, and then down again in response to a positive event.[11] This is how the adrenal system and cortisol are supposed to work. Once the fear or threat has passed, the body reregulates its cortisol levels. Yet, the children who had insecure attachments had no cortisol increase in response to a scary event. How could this happen?

The best way to understand this phenomenon is to think about living next to a really loud airport or train station. At first the noise bothers you, but after a while you get used to it and no longer jump out of your seat when you hear a roar or whistle. Your fear response has been "blunted" through acclimation. It is thought by various experts to be the same in children with insecure attachments. So used to the stress of always being on edge, their brains have become blunted and no longer produce cortisol under stress.

What we're talking about here is the deeper sense among children that they are safe and valued by their parents—the grown-ups who are the most important to their survival. When children are young, they cannot intellectualize this concept of value. They either feel it or they don't. When they feel it, they are more likely to trust others. When you are in trust mode, you are not in fear mode. As children get older, they build on this concept. Children who were raised feeling devalued are not going to trust many people or things; they will instead fear them. This very same fear can keep people distant from others, worried that they will be devalued again, and leave themselves even more vulnerable to the debilitating effects of fear itself.

——————— Exercise ———————

WHO INFLUENCED YOUR Ic?

Take a moment and think about the people who made you feel valuable in your home. Mom? Dad? Siblings? Grandparents, aunts, or uncles? How do you help your own children, partners, siblings, and parents feel valuable? Who do you like hanging out with more? Could it be because they do, indeed, remind you of your value? Here is a thought: Have you even considered that you have an opportunity to make your own parents feel valuable? When is the last time you actually thanked a parent for what he or she did? Take a moment today and, if you have a chance, let someone know how valuable he or she really is to you. Even a small token of appreciation can influence a person's mood and self-esteem, and make someone's day. As I like to say, a small change can have a big effect as we control no one but influence everyone.

————————————————————

Vulnerability and the Home Domain

Unless you can get your genetic representation into the subsequent generation, your lineage stops. Birds, reptiles, fish, and amphibians lay eggs outside their bodies. Some egg layers, like birds, may only have a very few eggs at a time, but then protect them from predators by literally sitting on them until they hatch. Most

▶ FEARFUL PARENTS AND PARENTAL FEAR

For many people, parenting is often the scariest journey on which humans embark and one in which all the domains of a person's I-M are widely stressed. How a parent behaves in relation to handling the stresses and fears of parenthood will have an impact early on in a child's development.

But what if those parents are already afraid? A study out of Johns Hopkins University School of Medicine looked at parents with social anxiety. These parents had an Ic where they did not feel easily accepted in the social domain themselves. Sadly parents with social anxiety were more critical of their own kids, were more likely to doubt that their kid was capable and competent, and were basically less snuggly and supportive.[12]

Insecure parents who have an Ic in which they see themselves as bad or inadequate caregivers keep it to themselves. This anxiety interferes with and delays getting their kids medical or psychiatric help when needed[13] and can create a self-fulfilling prophecy where the parent really does provide inadequate care. Once again, fear inhibits behaviors, in this case seeking help for a sick child. In their worry that they are not a good enough parent, they may create their worst nightmare—delaying treatment for their kid and then ironically being judged as an inadequate and bad parent.

other egg layers, however, have a strategy in which they lay dozens if not hundreds of eggs, hope that some of them are not eaten right away, and that others hatch and survive long enough to lay eggs of their own.

But mammals have evolved a very different approach. Instead of having our babies develop outside our bodies, mammalian babies at first develop inside the mother's uterus. Technically called "internal gestation," this evolutionary leap was a game changer in mammalian development. Some mammals, like dogs, cats, mice, and rabbits to name a few, may give birth to "litters" of babies— four, five, or more. But this is extremely rare in humans.

Because we had relatively so few offspring, most of whom died, human anxiety about infant survival may also have increased in proportion. We created protective dwellings, homes, to keep out predators. Yet this deep unconscious and evolutionary vulnerability leaves us vulnerable to news about human predators lurking just outside our doors, waiting to harm our children and jeopardize their well-being and our investment. We do not have to experience that horror, just be told it is there.

When I was growing up, it was the rare occasion when I was not playing outside. My wife has made the same observation. Neighbors kept an eye on each other's kids, and no one worried about the "liability" of kids cutting across their yards or playing on their property. There was an unspoken neighborhood watch, and most of us grew up in the relative safety of a friendly community. At nightfall, we quickly finished up whatever game we were playing and rushed home for dinner. Perhaps as a kid I was naive as to my parents' worry, but the "fear of strangers" did not seem to translate into a fear of predators looking to abduct one's child. My parents were not afraid of predators, so neither was I.

Back in 1977, Stanley Rachman not only suggested vicarious fear, but even more insidious, the generation of fear through information.[14] Today, with Amber Alerts, missing kids on milk cartons and billboards, and the plethora of TV crime shows, we perceive things differently. Whether it's based on reality or not, we have a greater fear of something happening to our kids than ever before. As a result, children's mental and physical development has changed. In fact, parents who are afraid of strangers impose greater restrictions on outdoor play of their kids, and those kids have, not surprisingly, a greater fear of strangers. Kids who play outside seem to have less fear of strangers. These findings from a study conducted in San Diego, Cincinnati, and Boston demonstrate a link between fear of stranger danger and the amount of physical activity of a child or teenager.[15] So not only are some kids getting less free, outdoor playtime, which is good for their physical health, they are also pumped with fears about being abducted.

One Fear Can Breed Another

Not unexpectedly, kids respond with fear when told about scary things. But what is a scary thing? Something dangerous, unpredictable, and uncontrollable. All of these attributes lead to mistrust. We often fear what we cannot control. This is well illustrated in a study out of England in which the most commonly reported fears of children ages five to sixteen were animals, blood/injections, and the dark.[16] But fear can generalize, seeping out of one object and being attributed to another. When 258 children between the ages of four and twelve years old were taught to fear an unknown dog-like animal, those kids also began to fear dogs and other predators.[17]

I have seen friends of my kids become terrified when our poodle, the friendliest dog in the world, barks in greeting. One guest had attributed a past negative experience to our dog.

This happens in small ways all the time. Most information of childhood is designed to develop basic skills. Hygiene is important from a survival point of view. Our parents inform us to brush our teeth or we will get cavities or have bad breath that will make us unpopular. Basic safety is important for survival, so we are told things like look both ways before we cross the street and don't play with matches. Tools and even playthings carry instructions. We are told not to touch hot stoves and boiling water, the dangers of swimming pools, or even of swimming too soon after a meal. Innocently, we receive information that is intended to protect us, but may unwittingly reinforce our vulnerability in the world. And vulnerable people are fearful people, because they begin to believe they do not have what is needed to survive.

Fabian: An Unhappy I-M

Fabian, one of my patients and a senior in high school, had performed poorly academically in the eleventh grade. His self-image as a scholar was profoundly damaged, and he feared he would not get into a good college. Not getting into college would place him at a disadvantage in getting a good job, which would place him at a disadvantage at having the family and security he hoped for as an adult. It also meant he would not be able to easily leave home.

His parents were all over him, restricting his cell phone and car privileges, demanding he get his college essays done, and watching him like a hawk for any deviation from their plan to get him through senior year on the honor roll. But the more they pressed him, the more inadequate he felt, the more fear he experienced, and the less productive he became. The less productive he became, the more his parents stepped up their control, which lead to a spiral of defeat where no one felt particularly happy. Small changes can have big effects, and it is through these small ways parents may unwittingly undermine their child's sense of value by generating fear in their kids. Through the eyes of his parents, this boy began to see himself as a failure—a person who let down not just others but himself as well. In their efforts to help, these parents had unwittingly rendered their son to feel as inadequate as he did. And as his fear increased, he became angrier with his parents, escalating the difficulty in applying for colleges.

The answer for Fabian and many other students in a similar predicament is to use the I-M Approach and recognize that, for whatever reason, the best he could do was screw up eleventh grade. As he began to explore the four domains, he acknowledged he had taken on many more honors classes than he could really manage. But afraid to disappoint his parents, as he realized himself, he did not ask for help but tried to muscle through his difficulty. As he got deeper in academic trouble, his anxiety increased and it became even more difficult to concentrate. So he started to get high on marijuana, which certainly did not help his academics. As his grades continued to plummet, his parents became more anxious.

Let's look at how Fabian's story illustrates how the domains of his I-M interact. At home his parents had expectations that he wanted to meet. His Ic domain wanted them to see him as successful and amazing. As such he took on an intense academic load in his social domain, wanting his teachers to also see him as successful and amazing. But under the stress of the academic workload, his cortisol level likely elevated, leading him to feel increasingly anxious and fearful. With all that cortisol, there was no way he could concentrate on math when the limbic system of his biological domain was convincing his PFC that he was in danger of being eaten by a saber-toothed tiger. Fabian began to withdraw, fearing that his parents were disappointed in him. Rather than be seen as unsuccessful in his Ic domain, he chose to worry alone, and this flawed strategy began to have repercussions in the other domains.

One of the basic rules I teach everyone, based on a wonderful book by Samuel Shem entitled *The House of God*,[18] is never worry alone. Parents have an opportunity to articulate this valuable rule, and not just live it by example. For most of our childhood, we have parents to worry with, but I do not recall my parents ever actually saying that to me. It was implicit but not put into those precise words. As parents, we have a chance to actually say this to our kids: "Never worry alone."

Fearful Home Domains and the Negative I-M

The vast majority of the time, parents are truly astonished that what they think is encouragement is perceived as criticism, leading to a child who may withdraw from the very help the parent is honestly trying to impart. Fabian, who was worried about college, is a great example. But there are other ways parents may influence their kids to fear, and create a home domain that negatively impacts a child's I-M.

▶ **MUNCHAUSEN SYNDROME BY PROXY**

A number of years ago, I was consulted by a pediatric team on an eleven-year-old boy who was about to undergo his fourth exploratory surgery for a series of symptoms described by his mother. She was a delightful person, always bringing candy and cookies for the medical team treating her son in the hospital. It seemed inconceivable that she would be making up symptoms in her child. But in fact, that was what she was doing. The boy's symptoms just didn't make sense. There was no reason for his constant vomiting, and the surgical team was stumped. Did he have some weird obstruction or was he unable to digest certain foods? Fortuitously, one of the overnight nurses walked in to check on him, thinking he and his mother who slept there every night were asleep. To her astonishment, the nurse found the mother pouring ipecac, a medicine used to make people vomit, into the boy's water jug at the side of his bed.

Perhaps the most extreme example of when anxious parents foster anxiety in their own children is a psychiatric disorder called "Munchausen syndrome by proxy." This is when a parent pretends the child has a serious medical illness and seeks attention for the child, often repeatedly. Thankfully, it is a very rare condition, but it is, therefore, poorly understood. These parents nearly always have some serious psychiatric conditions of their own. Serious psychiatric illnesses do affect some parents; nevertheless, this is an I-M. This unfortunate boy's mom did, indeed, have this psychiatric condition and his surgery was cancelled.

Arguing and Fighting

Tommy hated it when his parents went out at night. His eight-year-old body would tremble, his palms would sweat, his heart felt like it was going to burst out of his chest. His biological domain responded to the idea of being with a babysitter as if a predator was stalking him as prey. He would cry and grab at his parents as they extricated themselves from his grasp, just trying to go out for dinner.

It was the same when he was being dropped off for school. Separating from his mother was torture, for both of them. The vice-principal and the school counselor would try to intervene, but Tommy would push away their grasping hands and try to escape again to his departing mom. Feeling more and more inadequate, she sometimes would not even respond to him, turning her back even as the vice-principal would lift up the little boy and carry him back to the classroom, humiliating him in front of his peers.

Tommy came from a home in which his parents fought regularly. This is not infrequent parental behavior. Human beings do not always agree. But little children may not understand why their parents are fighting. They feel powerless to stop the fighting, and fear that their parents will be too busy fighting to protect the child. Tommy was one of those kids, and the thought of being alone ignited his fear to an all-consuming blaze.

The first few times Tommy came to see me, his mom had to stay in the room. Just the thought of her leaving increased his anxiety to the point where he would hyperventilate. When his mother did leave the two of us alone, Tommy would have to check the waiting room several times a session to be sure she was still there.

But after repeatedly satisfying himself that she was, indeed, still there, he would be able to tolerate having the door closed and chatting with me. Slowly Tommy began to recognize that his fear of losing his mom was just that: a real fear, but not based in any reality. She was outside the door of my office even if he couldn't see her. And she would be there at home when he came back from school. Every time Tommy's limbic system activated and he began to feel afraid, he would follow the Four Rs to reduce anxiety: recognize, rate, remember, reflect.

Tommy also began to recognize that his parents were not fighting because of him, nor was it his job to stop their fighting or protect his mom, as much as he wanted to. Tommy and his parents were all at their own I-M. This is not about blame but the reality that what we do has an influence on someone else. It was never his parents' intention to create anxiety in Tommy, but it did nonetheless.

We know much more about the long-term impact of growing up in a home with this degree of conflict. The most important thing parents can do is remind their kids that both Mom and Dad love them, and will always love them, even if they may not love each other as much now as they did before. Just because grown-ups grow apart does not mean that parents will stop loving their kids. As simple as this may seem, just speaking about this out loud with a child will go a long way in calming fears of kids at any age.

The I-M and Abuse
Claudia and I were in the middle of a session when a car backfired outside. Claudia startled. She began scanning the door to my office, as if someone were going to walk in and hurt her. It took several minutes for her biological domain to settle down so we could go on with our session. Claudia began to talk about the fear she experienced as a little girl, waiting to hear the front door slam, the heavy footsteps of her father striding up the stairs, the thrusting of the door being flung wide open to her room, and her father hurting her in many horrible ways.

Earlier in the chapter, I focused on some of the innocent ways parents can communicate fear to their children. But in my profession, I work with another group of people: children, adolescents, and adults who were physically or sexually abused by their parents, siblings, or other relatives. For many, their I-M is one of open emotional wounds from painful memories that intrude into their daily lives and interfere with school, work, relationships, and just being alive.

They are remarkable heroes who have survived terrible trauma, an affront to their Ic domain that no person ever deserves. In therapy and their everyday lives, they strive towards a different I-M, where their open psychic wounds can become scars—an emotional testimony to the battles they have survived. Often I will say that if anyone asks them to "get over it," my advice is to tell them to "Go to hell!" There are some things we never get over. But we have to come to terms with them to move forward to a different I-M.

This is one of the most difficult parts of the I-M Approach: *Everyone* is at an I-M. The abused and neglected, as well as the one who is abusing and neglecting. I am not suggesting forgiveness, although there are many fascinating studies on the power of this very human ability. But I am suggesting that both the person who is harmed and the person doing the harm are at their I-Ms. I don't have to like the behavior nor condone the behavior. I will hold the abuser responsible for his or her actions, just as the abused is responsible for his or her reaction, but I will respect both, acknowledging yet again that liking and respecting are two different things.

For my patients, it is at first very, very difficult to see the person who abused them as being at an I-M. This response is in part due to the anger and sometimes hate that the abused feels toward the abuser. But there is another component, one that gets to the core of many people who struggle with having been abused: self-doubt. They have self-doubt because most children who are abused do not say, "Why did you hurt me?" They say, in effect, "What did I do? I have an intact Theory of Mind, and through my Ic domain I see that the person hurting me sees me as some- one who deserves to be abused. There must be something wrong with *me*, as this other family member, part of my intimate group, is meant to protect me. I must have no value." It can take years for people who were abused to recognize that being abused had noth- ing to do with their value, but with the I-M of the abuser. The best *that* person could do was be abusive, based on the influence of his or her own four domains.

However, as people begin to recognize that they do have value, they can begin to wonder what was going on in the abuser's life to produce that I-M. Claudia began to explore her father's own childhood, how he had been beaten by his father, neglected by his mother, kicked out of the house as soon as he turned eigh- teen, and how he had turned to alcohol as a way to fight off his own sense of inadequacy. She began to recognize that her father had never really felt loved, and had difficulty giving love as a re- sult. She could not forgive him immediately for what he had done to her, but she began to shift to a different I-M, one in which she rekindled her own sense of value and self-respect. Almost a year later, she told me she and her dad had finally spoken about what he had done to her. "He cried. I hugged him. He hugged me back." They were both at a different I-M.

Mongolian Gerbils and Other Scary Thoughts

When it comes to creatures with which we don't have any fa- miliarity, most thinking is scary thinking. What we think affects what we feel. But what we say can affect what someone else feels. In a fascinating study from the Netherlands, researchers at the Institute of Psychology of Erasmus University showed a cage of Mongolian gerbils to a group of mothers of eight- to twelve-year- old children. None of the mothers had ever seen gerbils like this before. Some mothers were told the animals were dangerous, and some were told they were exotic but very nice and friendly gerbils.

Then the moms were told that their kids were going to have to approach the gerbils. The moms were given time to prepare their children for, as the scientists said somewhat ominously, " . . . this confrontation." Kids whose moms were scared of the gerbils were, sure enough, scared of the gerbils as well, and showed this by being reluctant to approach the animals. But kids whose moms had been told the gerbils were exotic but safe had no problem approaching these unusual little critters.[19]

It really comes as no surprise that our home domain has such enormous influence. After all, this is where trust begins, with the first oxytocin rush of attachment between parents and infant. We all know intuitively that we have an influence on our kids. We teach them morals and values, right from wrong, good from bad, left from right, and up from down. But without meaning to, we may be teaching them things that can inhibit their exploration of the world, just as these moms did who were scared of Mongolian gerbils.

These moms did not do anything wrong. In fact, they did everything right. It would be a scary mom indeed who encouraged her child to approach a man-eating gerbil! We do teach kids to look both ways before they cross the street, not to speak to strangers, and to wash their hands and brush their teeth. But hidden within these warnings are the roots of mistrust, and those mistrusts can inhibit any human being from venturing out into a world of the unknown.

This is where the I-M Approach can be particularly useful. Each of those moms, kids, scientists, and Mongolian gerbils is at an I-M, their own current maximum potential. A mom could say, "Look, this unusual gerbil is not the kind you want to pick up. It likes to bite. But let's take a look at it anyway because it is really kinda cool." You set a limit with how much you should trust the gerbil, but send a message that, even so, the gerbil is worth understanding. Its aggression is not something you need to like or condone: the result of the aggression is that this gerbil will be less likely to be cuddled and snuggled. But the Mongolian gerbil is still something to be respected, "re" again, "spect" look, to be looked at again with interest rather than shunned with disdain.

When scientists purposefully tried to train children to approach or fear a fictitious animal, they were more successful than they imagined. Kids who had been trained to approach an animal asked more positive questions, while kids taught to avoid it sought more negative information.[20] This bias in information seeking has enormous implications. Let's say a parent has a bias toward a particular food, or car, or gender, or religion, or skin color. Children exposed to these biases are at risk of taking them on, as well as the fears they can elicit. But they will ask questions to perpetuate the fear of that object rather than ask questions designed to dispel that fear. Those kids whose parents were afraid of dentists were more likely to ask if a visit to the dentist would hurt than what kind of sticker or prize they would get at the end of the visit.[21]

Fear of Medical Procedures

Billy was scheduled for surgery. On his way to the operating room, his dad walked on the left side of the gurney. But on the right, dressed in a tiny bowler hat perched on top of an enormous growth of wiry, curly red hair, his face painted white with exaggerated silly eyes and a giant bulbous red nose, flopped a clown. His suspenders held up overlarge pants, he wore a multicolored shirt, and his shoes were almost a quarter the length of the gurney itself.

Billy was laughing and giggling, too distracted by the silliness to worry a whit about his upcoming operation. Going to surgery with a clown and a parent reduced the anxiety in children even more than premedicating with a mild sedative, or going with a parent alone, according to the Meyer Children's Hospital in Florence, Italy. The effect lasted even in the room where the children were going to be put under anesthesia.[22]

So what does this tell us about anxiety? The clown is a very familiar archetype, a social representation of humor, laughter, joy, and invulnerability. How many clowns have been hit on the head with a giant hammer, only to remain giggling and intact, perhaps squirting water from a fake flower on their lapel, or countering with a bucket of confetti thrown harmlessly on their fellow clown? Rather than be fearful of surgery, the children accompanied by this symbol of silliness instead become calm and perhaps more trusting themselves.

Fear can be communicated in many ways, even if the words you use are meant to be calming. For example, in a study of one hundred children ages five to ten years, children who were getting ready to have their blood drawn were more fearful when their parents tried to reassure them, as opposed to distracting them.[23] Treating the parents' anxiety along with their children resulted in kids being less anxious, even three years later.[24] The implication? Calm parents raise calmer kids.

Fear of Injury

Jenny always wanted to play field hockey. From the sidelines she would watch the girls from her school running up and down the field, smashing at the rivals' legs with their sticks, tripping, stumbling, falling, getting up, and running again. At home, she enthusiastically told her mom about her desire. After a long silence, her mom gently took Jenny's hand and told her a nightmare she had about Jenny getting hurt, her shins bruised beyond black. Just the thought of her lovely but fragile daughter playing sports terrified her. What if something actually did happen? "Jenny," her mom said lovingly, "this is not a good idea." The next time Jenny went to a game, she began looking more carefully at the shins of those girls. Even though covered with pads, she began to imagine the dark-blue hues underneath. She noticed how some of the girls would limp off the field. Jenny took the school sports permission slip out of her backpack, crumpled it up, and threw it in the garbage. She never went to another game.

Fear of injury from doing organized sports or anything else can be transmitted from parent to child. Parents of six-year-olds completed a survey that measured their fear of a child being injured in general, and whether they thought their kid would be at risk of injury if they played organized sports. They filled out the same survey three years later, when their child was nine. Their children were assessed at age nine, and then again at age eleven. Just like Jenny, who decided not to attempt field hockey, the kids of parents who feared injury were significantly less likely to engage in moderate to vigorous physical activity.[25]

I doubt that any of those parents had any intention of influencing their child to avoid all physical activity, but they seem to have done so. In our deep biological drive to protect our offspring, we may unwittingly create obstacles to their own productivity. In my practice, there have been parents who have maliciously inflicted great harm on their children, but the vast majority were, unfortunately, oblivious as to the potential consequences of their actions. Perhaps their limbic system, so driven by an ancient capacity to fear, had overwhelmed their PFC and the ability to project into the future the likely outcome of their behavior. But the vast majority of these parents, when they did become aware of what had happened, were able to address it without resistance or guilt, because their behaviors, too, were framed as an I-M. They reflected from a position of trust, and this enabled them to make different decisions and influence a different I-M in themselves and their kids.

——————— Exercise ———————

YOUR CHILDHOOD FEARS TODAY

In this chapter I have touched on just a few examples of how our home domain can result in acquiring fear. Dentists, animals, and disease are just a few. What about you? What fears do you harbor that stem from your childhood? What explorations have you decided not to take because of these subtle and unintentional messages? Parents unwittingly may be creating Mongolian gerbils with more frequency than they realize. I had a patient who wanted to play the clarinet, but her parents remarked unthinkingly that there were no musicians in the family. And while she never learned to play an instrument as a result, all of her kids do. She was determined not to let her own small fear inhibit the musical potential of her kids. Relax. It's an I-M, but now that you know about it, you can do something to correct it and move to a different I-M.

———————————————

Repairing the Home Domain

One of the gems I have learned over time is to truly accept people for who they are, not for who you want them to be. Until you can do this, you are always at risk of being disappointed, and this disappointment can lead to greater insecurity in the relationship. But as soon as you accept another person at an I-M, amazing things begin to happen. Of course, even before that, you have to recognize that you are also at an I-M, simply doing the best you can at that moment. Your anger, disappointment, sadness, and fear are that particular I-M. When you recognize your I-M, you can relax, begin to trust *yourself,* and be less afraid that you will be rejected or seen as a disappointment. It is when we *don't* recognize and accept our I-M that we embolden our fears.

▶ RATIONAL AND IRRATIONAL FEARS

I was talking with my sixteen-year-old daughter about what made her afraid. "Well, Dad, I have rational fears and irrational ones." Rational fears were based in some reality, like performing in front of an audience, or going out on a first date. But irrational fears were, well, irrational! For example, Becca told me that when she was younger she would close her eyes and hold her breath when we drove through a tunnel. "You know how there are those doors in the tunnel, Dad? I used to think a man would jump out of one and hurt my family." She knew then, even at age seven, that it made no sense, but she would close her eyes anyway.

She and I began to explore the root behind that fear. First, a tunnel usually only has one way in and another way out, unlike being confronted by a danger in an open space, where you have many directions in which you can run. And Becca was afraid someone would hurt her family, indicating that she loved, valued, and cared about us. That feeling was completely rational, to love us, but the fear of losing us led her to very irrational thoughts.

The vast majority of homes have resulted in amazing kids who are ready to explore the world from a position of respect, value, and trust. Just being aware of the little ways we activate tiny terrors and a rapid response moves us, and everyone around us, to a different I-M. Yet even though our home domain, our nest, our residence, is meant to be a source of trust and safety, paradoxically that very safety can be a source of fear: the fear that we will lose that source of safety! Fear, as we have explored in previous chapters, ultimately stems from concern that our value as viewed by others is diminished, and we are at risk of being kicked out of our nest. And yet at a point in their children's development, parents are meant to prepare their kids for just that: leaving home and venturing into the social domain.

4

Social Security

The Social Domain

"Fear is the main source of superstition,
and one of the main sources of cruelty.
To conquer fear is the beginning of wisdom."
—Bertrand Russell, *Unpopular Essays*

As Halloween rolled around in 1983, advice columnist Abigail Van Buren, known to her readership as "Dear Abby," was wont to remind everyone of the modern dangers of the "hallowed eve." In her column that week, titled "A Night of Treats, not Tricks," she warned people of the dangers lurking out there for children: "Somebody's child will become violently ill or die after eating poisoned candy or an apple containing a razor blade."

Ah, the old Halloween scare reminding us seasonally of the dangers "out there," outside the domains of self and home, and in the murky, unpredictable social domain. No matter what kind of home domain we all experience, we are alerted at a very young age to the dangers of the world. "Out there" may not be a very safe place, so we develop keen radar, a heightened sense of fear. Whether it be an urban, suburban, or country setting, there is always something or someone to fear. And this kind of fear can impact your I-M in completely unique ways because we spend a lot of time in our social domains. This is our work, school, the playground, the stores, the streets on which we walk, the political and social organizations we're involved with, the town in which we reside, and the country in which we live. Fear in the social domain sows a poisonous seed that permeates our imaginations, despite facts like safety records and guarantees of security.

Human beings love a good story. Ever since human beings began gathering around campfires, we have enjoyed this communal part of our culture and heritage, the benefits of being a social animal with a remarkable capacity for language. But sometimes, and perhaps more often than we realize, many of our stories exaggerate dangers—for entertainment value and to make money—to the point of encouraging irrational fears.

Exactly twelve Halloweens after Dear Abby's scare column, Ann Landers, who was Abby's sister, wrote that "there have been reports of . . . razor blades and poison in taffy apples and Halloween candy."[1] The sisters never retracted their view. But Dan Lewis, who wrote about the sisters, went on to say that people had little reason to be concerned about the fear of poisoned candy because, although there had been many reports of such terrible acts, they are "almost entirely the stuff of myth."[2]

Perhaps digging deeper than anyone else to finally debunk this creepy urban myth, Joel Best, then a professor of sociology at California State University in Fresno, looked at thirty years of claims about crazed Halloween poisoners and so-called "fruit tampering." In a *Los Angeles Times* interview, he said, "We checked major newspapers from throughout the country from 1958 through 1988, assuming that any story this horrible would certainly be well reported." In all, he found a total of seventy-eight cases and two deaths. (The deaths were tragically real, but one was a parent who murdered his own child for insurance money, and the other was accidental, having nothing to do with Halloween.) Further checking proved that the other seventy-eight cases were pranks to attract media attention.[3]

Best's favorite story was "the kid who brought a half-eaten candy bar to his parents and said, 'I think there's ant poison on this.' They had it checked and, sure enough, there was ant poison on it—specifically, on the end he had not bitten." As it turned out, the kid had anointed the candy with poison himself.[4]

Regardless of the validity of the reports, whether it's Halloween dangers, sexual predators in our neighborhood, invasions of diseases like the Ebola virus, or violence in our schools, media-induced fears are pervasive. Fear finds its way into our brains, where it festers, bouncing back and forth between our limbic and PFC systems as our bodies prepare us for these threats, as if they were on our doorstep, until we can evaluate the information and determine its validity. However, we have always lived with fears of external unknowns, and, whether these unknowns are the stuff of media fiction or arise simply from the unpredictability of our interactions with other people, the fear that's incited demonstrates the power of the social domain. It can feel like a full-time job to sort all this out and know what we can ignore and what really warrants action. My aim in this chapter is to help you do just that—learn to assess which fears have to do with real threats and which fears actually have more to do with fear of not having value, of being cast out into the wilderness without a tribe to protect you. You have more influence over the social domain than you may think, and thus more control over your I-M when you are in the outside world.

Stranger Anxiety or Rational Fear

Tracy's case was unusual. I'd met many patients who were self-described homebodies—people who liked being home and felt they didn't need to venture out very far from home. But Tracy's story was quite serious. She had lost her job as part of her former company's cutbacks and hadn't been able to find another job. Over time it became clear that she'd reached a point where she actually didn't want to leave the house. That's when she contacted me at the urging of her husband.

When she began treatment, we faced an uphill battle from the beginning. Getting to a session was an emotional ordeal for her. She would imagine herself opening the front door and walking out into a world of strangers. The thought of driving her car flooded her with a wave of terror. She imagined approaching cars barreling through the guardrails or purposefully swerving to hit her. The last time she had been in a shopping mall, she experienced a crippling panic attack for no apparent reason. Her husband or father had to get her to appointments with me.

After a few sessions, it became clear that Tracy had an overwhelming fear of being in public places where she felt exposed, trapped. To Tracy, these environments stimulated profound limbic fear, crippling her, paralyzing her, and forcing her to remain in her home. Given her fears and reactions, I diagnosed Tracy with panic disorder with agoraphobia. This is an anxiety disorder in which a person has attacks of intense fear of being in places where it is hard to escape, or where help might not be available. It can involve crowded places, like shopping malls, sitting in a car in traffic, crossing bridges, or just being outside alone. According to the National Institute of Mental Health, approximately 5.6 percent of adults develop agoraphobia at some point in their lives.

But what does that really mean? Why do people get agoraphobia? Did Tracy develop agoraphobia because she was afraid of people? To many people, agoraphobia seems to arise when crowds might cause a fear of being trampled or assaulted. At first, Tracy seemed to have classic agoraphobia. Whenever she would enter the grocery store, massive levels of cortisol and epinephrine would race through her body, and Tracy would experience the same amount of fear as if she were being chased through the sa-vannah by a dangerous, hungry predator. Her heart raced and she felt out of control. Sometimes she would have to push her basket over to the side and just leave the store. The experience caused her great distress, as hard as she pushed herself to overcome it.

Tracy began to use the I-M Approach during therapy to explore deeper into the sources of her fear. Being attacked in the mall really made no sense: it was possible that this could be a reflexive manifestation of her limbic illogic, but Tracy reflected that it was so unlikely that someone in a shopping mall would physically attack her that she didn't think this is what had kept her in the shackles of fear. Instead, it was a deep-seated fear that people in that crowd would look at her and view her as inadequate—that if anyone looked at her too closely they would see who she really was and reject her. The other people in the social domain—all strangers—influenced Tracy's sense of self, her Ic domain. She saw herself as disrespected through their eyes. And this perceptual rapid response would activate the flight branch of her fight-flight response. With a combination of insight-oriented therapy, anti-anxiety medication, and cognitive-behavioral therapy, Tracy was able to take back her confidence and change her I-M when entering the social domain.

▶ FEAR OF PUBLIC SPEAKING

Imagine a small group of early humans gathered around a fire used to cook their meat and keep away predators. Most every-one is telling stories at their turn, embellishing the facts to rivet their audience. My guess is that at least some of those primitive storytellers experienced then what so many people, including a number of my patients, experience to this day: performance anxiety and a fear of public speaking.

When a patient believes he will never get over his fear, it is harder for him to do so. I see this in patients with social fear, especially of public speaking. At first they truly doubt that the Four Rs (recognize, rate, remember, reflect) will work, a vestige of their negative thinking. But as they begin to have more success with the technique, and as they begin to really understand and use the I-M Approach, they begin to approach themselves and the world with less fear.

What you think affects what you feel. When you don't think treatment is going to decrease your worries, don't expect therapy to work.[5] This is called "outcome expectancy," yet another manifestation of our PFC ability to wonder about the future and anticipate the outcome of an event. Those who fear public speaking are imagining and believing that they will say something stupid and be laughed off the stage. Remember Jimmy who had a fear of throwing up in school? Memory is also a function of time. We remember things with the intention of drawing upon past experience to influence the choices we make in the present and anticipate the impact of those choices on our future. Our imagination about that future can be a powerful source of irrational fear.

But the brain is going to do what the brain is going to do. It is at an I-M. If you think you might not be good enough, don't be surprised that your powerful brain will convince you of just that. This finding alone may compel patients to appreciate just how commanding their brain really is, even if it means keeping them afraid instead of gaining confidence. Once again, fear itself can make it more difficult to attain the very thing a person wants: to feel less afraid.

Looked at one way, it should be no surprise that Tracy couldn't leave her home—the world can be a pretty scary place. We live on a planet with seven billion people, the vast majority of whom are complete strangers. Imagine that for a moment: you walk out of the familiarity of your front door into a world of strangers; you drive to work, or take the train, surrounded by strangers; depending on the size of your workplace, you remain surrounded by strangers. We are influenced by strangers our entire lives—people we will never really get to know.

The vast majority of us, however, do not get stuck in our homes in extremis like Tracy. We go to work, go to school, go shopping, and explore the vast potential of our social domain. We are all on a spectrum of comfort in the social domain—some love to explore and travel the world over, and some never leave their hometown—but we are all heavily influenced by the outside world, and no force is greater at creating and maintaining a high level of fear than the media.

—————— Exercise ——————

SOCIAL DOMAIN FEARS: WHAT'S YOURS?

This seems like a simple enough question: What are some places where you are alert or suspicious of fearful things? Think about the places you go and the thoughts that go through your mind. For instance, going to church seems like one of the safest places for a person to enter the social domain; what could there be to fear? For some people, lots of things. There are germs on the pews, you look stupid trying to find the page in the hymnal, you may fear God's retribution for your sinful thoughts during the service, or nobody will speak with you at the coffee afterwards. While these all may sound silly to you, when we talk about fear in the social domain, we are all affected to some degree. What you may laugh at may be a source of trepidation for others. One person's medicine may be another person's poison, but one person's comfort may be another one's terror.

Make a list of a few of the scary things that you emotionally attach to these places. I'll give you an example of things that I have experienced:

- School (e.g., not having finished homework)
- Office (e.g., being perceived as not smart enough)
- Parties (e.g., can't make small talk well)
- Movies (e.g., there might be someone with a gun)

Now, again, you may not be afraid of going to these places, but fearful and suspicious thoughts run deeply, and it's only by identifying them that we can discover how ridiculous or legitimate they really are.

You and Me-dia

Unless you live in some remote part of the world, chances are that you are in some way "plugged in," either through a smartphone, the Internet, television, or some form of print media. And as we learned in the introduction, the more we are exposed to the media, the more fear we are fed, with the mandate "If it bleeds it leads." If you're in television or radio, you need ratings; if you run a newspaper or magazine, you need circulation; if you're on the Web, you need click-throughs. The higher the ratings and the more clicks, the more advertising revenue you can earn. In order to do this, you have to grab someone's attention, and how do you do this? You tug hard on the limbic mind through sensational storytelling.

A good example of this is child abduction stories, which are especially rampant on the Internet. When I was a kid, we played outdoors all day long and nobody thought someone in a car would come by, offer us candy, and take us away. Did things like that happen? Yes, there were a few rare cases, but over the years the fear of abductions has grown highly disproportionate to the occurrence. In 1996, pediatricians at the Mayo Clinic in Rochester, Minnesota, conducted a study of parents' worries and nearly three-quarters of parents said they feared their children might be abducted. One-third of parents said this was a frequent worry—a degree of fear greater than that held for any other concern, including car accidents, sports injuries, or drug addiction. Yet the facts about child abductions don't merit such active concern.[6]

Every ten years or so, the U.S. Department of Justice conducts a study of missing child cases in the United States. The most recent, NISMART-2, was published in October 2002. Take a look at the numbers:

- Nearly 90 percent of missing children have simply misunderstood directions or miscommunicated their plans, are lost, or have run away.
- 9 percent are kidnapped by a family member in a custody dispute.
- 3 percent are abducted by nonfamily members, usually during the commission of a crime, such as robbery or sexual assault. The kidnapper is often someone the child knows.
- Only about one hundred children (a fraction of 1 percent) are kidnapped each year in the stereotypical stranger abductions you hear about in the news.

About half of these one hundred children come home.[7] There is no greater loss than that of a child, but of all the dangers to children in the world, this is way down on the list. But the end result of the mass reporting of each and every rare case is that parents are terrified their children will be snatched, and today kids are rarely allowed to play out of doors without adult supervision.

Another example of a fear reaction to an event freezing us in our tracks is one that hit home for me: the Boston Marathon bombing. In the hours and days after the tragic event, the fear of a next strike was palpable. But no one knew who posed the threat, so we could not fight. We did not know where the danger was coming from or where it could appear next, so we could not run. Instead we froze. Citizens were asked to stay in their homes. Schools cancelled classes. The city came to a grinding halt. Boston was in freeze mode. People were terrified. But within a few days, one suspected perpetrator was dead, the other apprehended, and the actual threat was over.

Yet the fear lingered on. Were the bombers part of a larger network of terrorists? Why weren't the FBI, the CIA, and the police, our protectors, more vigilant? What would happen at the next marathon or other sporting event? Even as I write this, the investigation is continuing, with revelations that the main bomber had been in and out of the United States, had been on a watch list, but a misspelling of his name may have allowed him to pass through the airports unnoticed. All of these new pieces of information are being relayed to the public through the media. And while the intent may simply be to impart information, the framing of that information is one that is not calming but at times, frankly, terrifying.

The bombing of the 117th Boston Marathon remains an enormous affront and insult to a day devoted to honest and global competition. But 116 previous races were not attacked (and I hope I can say that none have been attacked since). When we can use our PFC to appreciate that the vast majority of races have been safe, we can shift out of a limbic fear to a more rational approach.

And there is one more thing to remember. The bombs went off in front of a colorful array of international flags representing runners from all over the world. In an instant, runners and spectators were terribly injured, some lost their lives, but the majority of others ran, not away, but toward the injured, their natural limbic reflex to flee overwhelmed by their deep human reaction to help. Even though the media may instill fear in us, there is also the profoundly human desire to be part of a group, and to help the members of that group—a deep desire so strong it can overcome the most ancient of fears.

Do Terrorists Have an I-M?

I recently gave a talk on the I-M Approach to a group of Bostonians. A woman in the audience raised her hand and said in a relatively angry voice: "Dr. Shrand. Surely you are not saying that the marathon bombers were at an I-M. I have to respect that they killed and maimed dozens of people? How can *that* be an I-M?" Before I could reply, other voices echoed her point.

A middle-aged man spoke up. He had been in the runners' tent just past the finish line, helping competitors suffering from fatigue, replenishing their dehydrated biological domains with water and electrolytes. And then a bomb went off, and then another. He spoke about the surreal experience as he ran out of the tent to see dozens of people injured, his eyes tearing as he told us what he saw—and what he did.

The audience fell silent, expecting him to agree with them: How could those bombers be at an I-M? But then he said something remarkable. "I can't help wondering what would have happened if some small change had occurred years before. What if one of the bombers had not gone to Russia and been radicalized? What would have happened if one of the brothers had talked the other one out of it? What small change could have had an enormous influence? What if either or both of them had felt more valued by *our* group rather than a different group?

"I don't like what they did. I am certainly not condoning it. Both brothers are held responsible: one is in jail and the other is already dead. But I cannot help wonder why they did it. What was going through their heads? Why was this the best they could do, to hurt so many people? Why is this the best any terrorist can do? And do they even see themselves as terrorists or just a valued member of a different group, a group that does not value us and sees us as devaluing them? I was there. I pressed on people's arteries to stop the bleeding. I am angry, and when I go to a movie and a gun is fired or a bomb goes off [in a movie scene], my heart jumps and I want to run outside. But I think if I stay angry and afraid, I may not go back to the marathon next year. And I plan on going back."

This is one of the most difficult aspects of the I-M Approach: How are violence and crime, affronts to our social domain, an I-M? It challenges every moral fiber of our being. But this is what the I-M Approach asks of us: to wonder about the motivations of other people without judgment. Just as I am asking all of us to wonder about our own motivations, without judgment, so we need not fear what we may find and not dare to look at all.

———————— Exercise ————————

TEMPTED BY TABLOID, PFC POWER OVER MEDIA MESSAGES

While much of the information we get from the various sources of media we encounter can be useful, my guess is that at least half of what I see is geared toward grabbing my limbic system and squeezing it hard. Take a gander at these actual Internet headlines from a major "news" website. Which ones have you seen, been tempted by, or actually clicked on?

Diet Drug Recalled: Tampering Possible
Voicemail: A Clue to a Boy's Death
"OMG": Man Escapes Fire
Girl, 8, Abducted by Shelter's Janitor? (this headline actually has a question mark included)
People at Bus Stops See UFOs

See Cars Crash, Crash, Crash
Your CPAP Is Crawling in Germs

We're all tempted by tabloid headlines from time to time, as a distraction of sorts. But how do you feel afterwards? Probably pretty yucky and not very safe or trusting of other people. How could you? You've allowed something adverse, unpleasant, and scary to enter your brain space. When we only have a limited number of minutes, hours, and days in our lives, why choose to indulge the limbic space? You can choose not to. Don't click, don't watch, don't read. Your social domain I-M, no matter what's going on in the Ic and home domains, will be much better off for it.

———————————————

I am not advocating that we let down our guard to the point of being naively vulnerable. We cannot run into traffic without the risk of getting hurt. But the idea that we have to be on guard all the time is a sad vestige of our ancient limbic survival response, as if we had never left the jungle or savannah. Though we have left those environments behind, we have recreated our own concrete jungles and cement savannahs in which we perpetuate the basis of our fear. How would we defend ourselves against a predator? How do we stay valuable so we are not cast out of the group and at risk of being prey? The media have an answer for that as well.

Neuromarketing or Mind Control

Imagine one of our ancestors happening upon a mango tree. She reaches up and plucks the attractive looking orange-red fruit, and takes a bite. Instantly the delicious taste activates part of her brain, rapidly laying down a memory: "That was good!" she thinks. In her biological domain, she has created a sense of plea-sure, and the next time she sees a mango tree she will be more likely to approach it and look for another mango. And yet, despite this powerful reinforcement of pleasure, if she sees a predator lurking under the tree, she will forego that mango and run away.

This basic brain response, the assessment of risk, continues to influence many of our decisions. But if the brain is going to choose fear or pleasure, it will choose pleasure every time. Fear feels horrible, but pleasure feels great. In fact, feeling rewarded in some fashion is the basis of commerce, the way human beings trade their resources to gain other resources. This is what marketing is all about. Ever since human beings began to trade and barter for goods, the consumer has been at a potential disadvantage because of this desire to feel pleasure over fear. The Romans even coined a phrase, warning the consumer to be aware of unscrupulous tradesmen: caveat emptor, or buyer beware. Assess the risk.

In our commercial world of the twenty-first century, the ability to influence, and even manipulate, a potential consumer has now spawned a brain-based approach to tapping into what a person wants. Called "neuromarketing," this approach constantly uses information about our brains to design cereal boxes, cars, clothes, perfumes, and much, much more. Neuromarketing exploits our deeper understanding of the reward system in our brains. When you combine this with our human proclivity to want to be part of a group, it creates a powerful new tool for business called "consumer neuroscience."[8]

Consumer neuroscience (CN), and all marketing, is heavily reliant on our human desire to feel valued. Using our ability to compare sets of information, CN gets the brain to get a little anxious about making the wrong choice and becoming less desirable. This approach breeds mistrust, and with mistrust comes fear. Watch out! Better not buy the wrong pair of sneakers, the wrong car, the less-current smartphone. Make the wrong choice and the person who makes the right one is made out to be at a serious advantage: more likely to get the date, the job, the place of greater value in the group. True? Probably not. Caveat emptor applies as much today as it did in ancient Rome.

So it's not hard to figure out why marketers do this. The more they can understand and appeal to the inner workings of the human brain, the more stuff they can sell and the more money they can make. But why do people buy it? Why do they put stock in such a belief system? Why is the force to look good, smell good, not be bald, and be well shaven, perfectly highlighted, unwrinkled, and wealthy to boot so powerful in the social domain?

There's a simple answer to this question, and it's the same answer to most of our questions about fear: we are afraid of not being accepted by the group. The emotional appeal to human beings to be attractive to and accepted by the group is overwhelming to most people all over the world, not just in our Western culture. Just think about how important this is, especially for young people who are highly vulnerable to this kind of marketing because they are so obsessed with how they look, being cool, and fitting in—and everything they feel is so intense.

Is it any wonder that personal grooming is a multibillion-dollar industry and that teenagers and young adults are one of the greatest marketing targets. The teenage brain, because of the way it matures, has a limbic system more in control than the prefrontal cortex. As such, the teenager can be impulsive and emotional, wants to take risks, and seeks pleasure. (I am imagining a lot of parents reading this book nodding their heads right about now.) But as the PFC is maturing, the teenager also wants to be social. Peer pressure becomes overwhelming in many cases and appearance is critical.

People's tendency to judge a book by its cover or other people by the quality of their skin or the style of their clothing reflects a culture driven by a fear of not fitting in, of being viewed as somehow inadequate in comparison to the ideal state they're supposed to desire. This is how fear can inhibit us. The kids with acne are

> ▶ **ACNE VULGARIS: A COMMON HUMAN CONDITION**
>
> As common as acne is among teens, those kids and young adults who have it bad have been found to be at a significant disadvantage. Even the technical term, "acne vulgaris," makes a person with acne sound "vulgar" and offensive. A collaboration of scientists from Florida, Nevada, and Georgia created a computer program that could make a face look like it had acne or not. Research subjects were asked to view these faces and report their impression of that person, in other words report on the Ic domain.
>
> Compared to those with clear complexions, faces with acne were more likely to be rated by their peers as shy, nerdy, stressed, lonely, boring, unkempt, unhealthy, introverted, and rebellious.[9] The researchers also interviewed kids who actually had acne, most of whom reported being embarrassed by it and describing it as the single most difficult part of being a teenager. These kids had lower self-confidence, were shy, had difficulty finding dates, problems making friends, challenges at school, and trouble getting a job. And kids with acne were perceived as more likely to be bullied. They were definitely not in the protective graces of the group.

stifled in their ability to engage in some relationships, while kids who reject them are deprived of making a new friend. And even as they may shun the kid with acne, they perpetuate their own fear of waking with a pimple. Shrewd marketers prey on this fear, and teenagers then buy more and more products to ensure that they remain clear of acne.

Our social domain is one where fear finds fertile ground. If in our heart of hearts a human being simply wants to be valued by another human being, then the fear of rejection, of being devalued, may be worth investing in at almost any price. Being valued feels great; being rejected feels horrendous. It is this fear of rejection that has been used to promote the purchase of items from carrots to cars. In essence, we have become prey to these new predators lurking in the bushes of neuromarketing. But all of the people in these companies, from custodian to CEO, and all the consumers to whom they sell—all of them are at their own individual and unique I-M.

The Media and Politics: In-groups and Out-groups

Being part of a group carries with it enormous survival benefit. To remain part of that protective group, you have to have value, contribute, and then protect the group that offers you protection. You develop loyalty to your group and identify with your group, using your ability to compare sets of information by comparing your group to a different group. You are part of your "in-group," and not part of the "out-group." This group can be as small as a pair of lovers, but extend to larger groups like sports fans, brand loyalties, political and religious organizations, and many more.

But, while being part of a group is protective, one group can perceive that another group threatens that protection. Across the world, many nations have a division within their country: political parties. Fear and threat, therefore, may be driving forces for political systems that alienate and even vilify and denigrate those who do not conform. Perhaps there is no better example than the way competing politicians use the media to broadcast negative ads designed to instill fear in potential voters: a vote for the opponent is represented as a vote that will come back to haunt you with consequences a politician thinks you fear, e.g., higher taxes or fewer benefits. Thus fear can be used to divide a country, feeding on the old terror that marauding warriors from other tribal factions are just waiting to inflict harm.[10]

There are studies that help to clarify what these threats actually are that have induced the fear. A group out of New Zealand gave a ninety-three-item survey to 463 undergraduates, asking the students to rate their feelings of fear, concern, and anxiety. Five distinct fear-related factors were identified: harm to self, child, or country; personal and relationship failures; environmental and economic fears; political and personal uncertainties; and threats to the in-group.[11] Political leaders may exploit all of these broad categories to rally a group around them at the expense of another group. When one group feels victimized by another, anger can ignite retaliation and aggression, behaviors inhibited by fear.[12] The examples of using fear to suppress aggression from an out-group are rampant throughout history, and persist even today. On a daily basis, we can pick up a newspaper or read something on the Internet about some political regime suppressing the rights of other people. In the Middle East, the Arab Spring was a result of many people feeling oppressed. In colonial America, on the night of December 16, 1773, Samuel Adams and the Sons of Liberty raided three ships in the Boston Harbor, throwing 342 chests of tea overboard to protest unfair taxation by the United Kingdom.

Throughout history, story after story has been told about groups of people rising up or being squashed down by other groups of people. Today we read about them, receive instant messages about them, or may even be in one of those groups. The media can make us feel sorry for some of them as oppressed people, but also can instill in us a fear that our own culture may be the next one caught in the throes of revolution. Some political leaders rally people to act against discrimination, while others rally people to discriminate in the name of their own morality against issues like abortion or gay marriage. One group is led to fear the disintegration of *their* way of life when an out-group gets to live *their* way of life. Fear can be exploited to pit one group of humans against another, and the media can serve as a biased bully pulpit endorsing one view or another. Caveat emptor!

▶ **SEEING IS BELIEVING, BUT HEARING TAPS INTO THE IMAGINATION**

Is there a difference between watching a scary show and hearing about scary news? Researchers in the Netherlands think there is. Kids from nine urban primary schools, 572 of them between the ages of eight and twelve years old, were more scared by hearing violent news than they were by watching violent TV shows. Those kids in the Netherlands became more afraid that they would become victims of violence including murder, war, and house fires.[13] This is a fascinating piece of information. Human beings really are receptive to stories, just as if we were still huddled together and sitting around that protective fire on the savannah.

The sad thing is, this data has been around for almost ten years. How many of those kids are still more afraid, now in their late teens and early twenties? The social domain has intruded into our home domain in the form of television and now the Internet. But by the same token, the values and ethics we learn at home become enacted in the social domains of our schools, workplaces, streets, stores, and all the relationships with the people who live there and bring their own I-M to those interactions. If we are learning fear at home, there should be no surprise that we bring fear to the social domain, impacting our Ic and biological domains, and those internal domains of those around us. If we are fearful, we breed fear in others through the activation of mirror neurons and ToM.

Television or Terrorvision? The Effects on Adults

Being a grown-up is not an immunization against being scared by the media news. Researchers out of Towson University in Maryland surveyed 1,905 female undergraduates, trying to understand fear of rape. They found that the perception of harm and danger had more influence on fear than actual past violent experiences.[14] Women were more afraid of strangers, of not being strong enough to fight off an attack, and of attack at night. But one of the greatest fears was the long-lasting emotional damage, and the social stigma that haunts a person who has been raped. The Ic domain is so powerful that a person who has been violated worries still that other people will in some way reject or avoid them.

Invisible Dangers Are Just as Scary: Fear of Germs

For tens of thousands of years, visible predators were the danger that caused us to fear. The Western world had known about "little animals," miniscule single-celled creatures first observed by the father of microbiology, Anton van Leeuwenhoek, in the 1650s. Yet, it was inconceivable that something so small could pose any danger. But two hundred years later, in 1876, Robert Koch established that these microorganisms could invade your body and cause disease that could maim, kill, and be spread all too easily from person to person to person. Small changes really could have big effects.

For most of our cultural existence, however, human beings had no idea about our fellow microbial companions inhabiting the world. When a person came down with a fever or developed some change from "health" to "illness," we called in shamans and tribal healers. Our brains could not conceive that an animal so small it was essentially invisible could enter our bodies and possibly kill us. So we made things up in explanation. We attributed the sickness to some invading spirit or a spell cast by an angry, vindictive competitor.

But now we know about germs, viruses, and other infectious organisms that penetrate our biological domain. We know what we need to do to have power over these tiniest of animals. In the United States, pretty much every bathroom in a restaurant has the ominous warning sign, "Employees must wash their hands."

We cajole our children from a very young age to do the same, subtly inducing in them a fear of these most minuscule of creatures that can be the cause of such enormous destruction.

A mother came to my office extremely worried about her five-year-old son, Roger. He was not as affectionate since he started kindergarten, refusing her hugs, not wanting to hold her hand when they crossed the street, not even wanting her to kiss him good night. She was terrified something had happened to him at school—perhaps, she dreaded, sexual abuse. Thankfully, nothing like that had transpired. What had happened was that in Roger's first health class, he learned about germs. His teacher told him how they can jump unseen and invisible from one person to another—by touching.

I suppose she was trying to be helpful, teaching these five- and six-year-old kids how to prevent the spread of disease. But what she really imparted was an irrational fear of contamination. Fear followed Roger home, and for the next year he would not give his family a hug nor let them touch him, for fear of these invisible terrors.

In fact, Roger became so afraid of germs that he would take several baths a day and brush his teeth in the hallway so that his toothbrush would not be contaminated by anything in the bathroom. This was not a contamination fear associated with obsessive-compulsive disorder. Roger was responding the best he could to the imagined dangers of the unseen world of germs. Of course his response made perfect sense in the world of a five-year-old, who was at his I-M. The unforeseen benefit was that Roger, of all this mother's kids, has the best teeth! In fact, many years later, his mom told me a story that one of her friends had complimented Roger on his smile and said to him, "I wish I had your teeth," to which this relatively concrete-thinking preadolescent said politely, "Sorry. I'm using them."

Germs are now part of our life. We are fully aware of the

danger, reminded on an almost daily basis, by the media or just a sign in a restaurant restroom, that we can be infected at any moment. AIDS, hepatitis, strep infections, staph infections, MRSA (bacteria that can't be killed by regular antibiotics), the common cold. We learn that germs and parasites lurk in impure water or undercooked food. We hear about polio and cholera, and read with horror about the Black Death that swept through Europe between 1348 and 1350, killing seventy-five to two hundred million people. We have worried about swine flu, avian flu, the biological weapons reportedly used by Syria in the Arab Spring of 2013, and the deadly viruses like anthrax waiting to be released by terrorists—groups of people who have decided that our group is a threat to be taken out.

So we take pains to keep ourselves safe. We disinfect a scrape on the knee or a cut from a kitchen knife. We teach our kids to cover their mouth with the crook of their arm before they cough or sneeze, and to wash their hands before eating a meal. In the United States, we are encouraged to get our flu shots every winter. People can call their pharmacy and get a recorded message reminding them that they can come in to get their immunization for free.

Researchers from the Sol Price School of Public Policy in Los Angeles wanted to find out the toll of being barraged by media that bellow these warnings on a regular basis. First, the scientists made up fifteen days' worth of local "news" about the outbreak of a potentially deadly virus. They then took three hundred people from Los Angeles and three hundred from Washington, DC, and showed them the news clips over fifteen days. Some subjects were told the virus was on the opposite coast, others that the virus was approaching their neighborhood.

As the virus got closer, the fear went up. Some of the people were told that the virus had escaped in a lab error, some that it had been released by a terrorist—both pretty scary prospects. But some subjects were told that no one had any idea of the source or type of virus. They were in the dark, but just knew a very deadly virus was getting closer and closer. Compared to those who thought the virus was from a lab error or terrorist attack, the people who had no idea where the virus had originated had fear that was through the roof![15]

One way to interpret this finding may be a basic belief that labs try to be safe and our government is trying to protect us from terrorist attacks. But when the source is unknown, our desire to run away increases. The problem is we don't know where to run so we may freeze, try to become invisible, and hope the danger passes us by, just like the city of Boston shutting down in the wake of the marathon bombing. The freeze response in this case, however, doesn't work, because the virus is on its way, getting closer to where you are. In this case, the flight response becomes active, and our avoidance behavior makes us take leaps and bounds to escape.

This dramatic response is elicited from a television show, a controlled exposure of subjects by researchers to the perception of a threat. Once again, what we think affects what we feel. Our imagination is a remarkable source of creativity, and an unfortunate source of sometimes crippling fear. Perhaps our limbic brain does not always "know" that what we are thinking about may be based in fantasy and sees it as reality. When we do not know the source, we have less chance of diverting the danger, or of running away. This applies to theoretical studies like the one on the imaginary virus, or those insidious unconscious messages that have become embedded in our perception of little fears every day. But even when we do know the source, our fears can get the better of us. For example, a lethal outbreak of the Ebola virus in Uganda, Africa, set off some real fears and some very unrealistic fear responses.

The Ebola virus is truly horrible and terrifying. A person can be going about his business when, out of the blue, he is hit with what looks like a severe case of the flu. He can barely move, he feels so tired. Achy joints and muscles, sore throat, cough, headaches, difficulty breathing, and one weird one: many get severe hiccups. A person infected with Ebola looks like any other flu victim, until—like some sufferers—he develops confusion, agitation, seizures, or even goes into a coma. Ebola causes intense stomach pain, diarrhea, and vomiting. The virus attacks the blood itself, destroying red blood cells that burst open, leaking their contents into the skin, causing bruises, blood blisters, and massive rashes. What a terrifying disruption of the biological domain!

An outbreak of the Ebola virus in Uganda occurred between September 2000 and February 2001. Scientists found the two main English-speaking newspapers in Uganda carried 639 articles, editorials, cartoons, and letters from around the world responding to the Ebola outbreak. Confusion, anger, and stigma were accompanied by articles about medical staff working themselves to exhaustion, patients running away from hospitals, appeals to "spiritual forces" to protect against infection, a demand for a national control strategy, and international travel restrictions.

Such a response suggests Ebola was a modern plague, with hundreds of thousands of people infected and dying from a massive outbreak of this horrible disease. But in reality, 425 people developed the disease. Granted, more than 50 percent of them died, which speaks to how deadly Ebola truly is. But the global response seems to be quite dramatic and perhaps out of proportion to the actual danger.[16] If it bleeds it leads, and Ebola was reported as a disease that basically exploded the blood inside your body until there was no more blood to explode.

Immunizations Are Not Immune from the Media

In our attempt to live in a safer world, we may have inadvertently supported the view that the world is actually not safe. As our knowledge about all the things that can kill us increases, we

▶ TELEVISION AS A TOOL FOR PUBLIC HEALTH

Fear can also be used for social good. In 1982 cyanide in Tylenol bottles killed seven people, leading to the safety caps and sealed medicine bottles we are so familiar with today. Tighter airport security is a direct response to the terrorist attacks of 9/11/2001 that killed nearly 3,000 people. Seat belt laws, speed limits, and strict penalties for drunk driving are in response to the more than 30,000 driving-related deaths in the United States each year.

The antismoking campaign has probably saved millions of lives and billions of dollars in health care savings. These antismoking messages can even be culturally targeted, with excellent results. For example, antismoking campaigns have been designed targeting New Zealand Maori and American Indians. Culturally specific messages were much more effective in decreasing smoking than generic fear campaigns.[17] When marketing taps into someone's social domain and their resultant Ic identity, the message becomes more "personal" and more influential as a result.

A recent spate of celebrity deaths from drug and alcohol overdose has drawn attention to this public health crisis. As a result, our nation is moving away from seeing addiction as a moral issue to seeing it as a medical issue, one deserving attention from one of the best health care systems in the world. Parents' fears for their children, spouses' fears for their spouses, and patients' fears for themselves, swept up in the throes of addiction, have started an inspiring momentum. Instead of hating addicts, the media are helping us hate addiction and bring the person whose I-M is using drugs back into the social domain, rekindling their sense of value and trust.

There is nothing wrong with fear. It is what you do with it that matters. In this case, fear can be used to get across a public health message. Fear is an emotion designed to make you

stop: stop and think if you should really smoke that next ciga-
rette or experiment with that drug. But it is still sad that our
brains sometimes need to be scared and limbic to do something that our prefrontal cortex should just recognize is common sense. But it is an I-M.

become ever more vigilant. In some cases, this awareness leads to an intersection of medicine and the law, for example in restric-tion against drunk driving on our roads and the requirement for carbon monoxide detectors in our homes. However, when sci-ence and the media get it wrong, there can be misinformation that spreads like wildfire.

Perhaps one of the most famous and debilitating examples of this started with a 1998 paper by Dr. Andrew Wakefield. Based on a review of only twelve children who had received a measles, mumps, and rubella vaccination (MMR), he published a paper suggesting a link between the vaccination and the development of autism.[18] The idea blazed through the autism community and fueled the uncertainty of many, many parents faced with protect-ing their children from a preventable infectious disease but poten-tially increasing the risk of a lifelong threat of autism. As such, a large number of infants were not immunized, causing an increase of measles and its complications in the general population. This surge became a public health crisis in the United Kingdom, the United States,[19] and many other countries, all the result of par-ents becoming scared to vaccinate their children based on media-driven publication of one paper looking at twelve children.

The paper was thoroughly discredited through scientific stud-ies, and the publishing journal, *The Lancet,* one of the most re-spected medical journals in the world, published an editorial letter saying they were formally retracting the article.[20] Even so, a recent study has resurrected the idea that immunizing your children with vaccinations may cause autism, perpetuating the controversy.

Polio has been virtually wiped out. Parents can access immunizations against measles, mumps, and rubella—illnesses that used to rip through communities before the vaccine. With concerted medical effort and public health messages, our society can protect itself against at least some of the more common infectious diseases like measles, mumps, and rubella. But if we let our irrational fear responses take charge, we may deprive ourselves of some of the easiest ways to protect ourselves against bacteria that are really just at their own I-M when they infect our biological domain.

There's Nothing Wrong with Fear; It's What You Do with It

Our society has subtly, perhaps innocently, used fear as an instrument of motivation. Sometimes the consequence is a kid who won't give you a hug, and sometimes it's a kid who doesn't need a dentist. But fear is influential either way. The mechanism is the same: fear inhibits our ability to move, limbically cajoling us to remain still and wait until the danger passes. But an entire society of paralyzed people like Tracy, who couldn't leave her home, would not survive for very long. Our brains have had to find some way to tolerate this unconscious and relentless fear.

One way employed by our social domain is to modulate fear by framing it as a way to enhance our survival. Fear is subtly packaged by our social domain. For example, fear has been used to teach about the dangers of smoking cigarettes, driving drunk, not washing your hands, or forgetting to brush your teeth. We take what may be a legitimate fear and offer a way for you to overcome that potential danger. The medical profession and public health initiatives have parlayed the fear of lung cancer into improved

▶ FEAR OF CANCER CAN BE USED FOR EARLY DETECTION ... BUT NOT ALWAYS

Cervical cancer affects about eight out of every one hundred thousand women in the United States. An estimated 12,360 women will be diagnosed, and 4,020 of those women are sadly expected to succumb to the condition every year.[21] Early detection is key to early intervention, which leads to a significantly greater success rate. In a study out of Belgium, researchers showed that education about cervical cancer heightens awareness and the perception of risk. Five hundred women ages eighteen to eighty-five were asked how many times they had seen television messages about cervical cancer.[22] Those women occasionally exposed were twice as likely to be very afraid, frequently exposed three times as likely to be both very and extremely afraid, and those regularly exposed were also three times more likely to perceive a moderate risk and seven times as likely to perceive a large risk of being diagnosed with cervical cancer. The researchers suggest that television ads, therefore, are an effective means for educating the populace about health-related subjects.

The study did not explore, however, how this fear translated into women going for regular Pap smears, the main diagnostic tool used to assess cervical cancer. Indeed, fear itself may inhibit a woman from going to a doctor for a Pap smear, according to an earlier 2009 study out of Michigan. In a review of other research papers from 1994 to 2008, Drs. Kelly Ackerson and Stephanie D. Preston found that women who feared medical examination, providers, tests, and procedures, or did not seek knowledge about cancer, were less likely to go for treatment. But women who did have knowledge, feared cancer, and trusted their care providers were more likely to get treatment.[23]

health. This group has investigated a myriad of potential dangers and a myriad of ways to defend against them.

Some of these dangers are individual, like smoking cigarettes. But we now know that secondary smoke is also dangerous to another person sharing the direct social domain of the smoker. As such, some societies have adopted new rules, leading to things like smoke-free restaurants and other establishments. Once a danger is determined to potentially impact more than one person, rules become a powerful modality to address these social fears. To have the best chance of defending against dangers that can impact an entire group, our social domain develops certain rules for everyone to follow.

Rules Rule

The majority of my patients fear that in some way they have broken some basic expectation of their home or social domain, that their Ic is one of vulnerability and inadequacy, and that they are not worthy of respect. Some become sad, some become angry, but at the heart of these feelings is a fear that they are not seen as valuable by members of their group. Some kids break their curfews, others don't even bother to go out and socialize. All of the kids I see in my substance abuse program have broken the rule of not doing drugs or alcohol. Some of them have committed crimes like stealing, vandalism, and physical assault. The kids who have been caught in a crime may come to treatment rather than go to jail.

Teenagers, with a limbic system more in control than the PFC, often appear impulsive, even though they are at an I-M, their maximum, given the development of their brain. Yet these impulses often result in the breaking of a rule, a violation of a social expectation. A kid may skip school, not go to bed on time, jump off a roof on a skateboard, or drive over the speed limit. We grown-ups consider some rules just common sense. Some stem from religious or legal traditions, such as the Golden Rule: do unto others as you would have them do unto you. Some rules evolve and give way to social evolution, like women being able to vote, equal rights, and gay marriage. Some cultures do not adhere to the same standards as other cultures, but all of them have rules.

When enough people agree to these basic rules, we may call them "laws." The vast majority of laws are designed to maintain some form of respect, and when that respect is violated, the violator is at risk of an entire group of people rallying together to hold her accountable. The legal system has used the fear of jail and punishment as a way to enforce the rules. Some cultures forgo the western judicial system and enforce the rules through tribunals run by local leaders, or by religious authorities. No matter the social structure, however, rules represent a shared set of social standards that serve as guideposts to behaviors.

The origin of these rules, however, may be based in fear. When we were first forming social groups, rules created a shared expectation. In a scary world, rules can be a source of predictability and calm: if someone breaks the rule, he will be held accountable and have to repay some debt to the person harmed and the social group as a whole. A rule is dependent on our ability to anticipate a consequence: if I do something now, something will happen later in response. Once again, the advent of our PFC creates a means for us to allay our limbic fear. Rules are very much influenced by Theory of Mind and our ability to compare sets of information. ToM provides an ability to measure how well other people think we are adhering to the rule, and this measurement is enforced by comparing adherence to or deviation from the rule. Adherence to the rules increases the chances we can stay in the group, while deviation from those rules increases the chances of some retribution from the group, including our worst fear, exclusion.

Following the rules of the home and social domains, recognized and responded to through Theory of Mind and the Ic domain, enhances our chances of staying in that group. Being part of a group reduces the biological domain fear of vulnerability and becoming prey. But as a result, we fear being kicked out of that group and losing the protective mantle of our place in society. President Roosevelt had it right when he talked about social security. But now we know how evolution and formation of our brains has allowed us to even live in a group at all.

Fear and the Afterlife

The development of the PFC, the prefrontal cortex, and our ability to anticipate the future brought with it an unanticipated consequence: an awareness of time. Memory is the ability to preserve a present moment for retrieval in the future and the retrieval of a past moment in the present. This has enormous survival advantage, allowing our ancestors to remember where a fruit-bearing mango tree was, or recognize the telltale snap of a branch or rustle of a thicket that suggested a prowling predator. This understanding of time, combined with Theory of Mind, promoted the development of altruism, where I give something to you now with the unspoken promise that you will return the favor in the future. To ensure this, sometime in the future I would have to retrieve a memory of the past altruistic act to ask for the return of the favor in the present.

The perception of time has become a critical part of our survival. Being able to anticipate the consequence of my action allows me to execute better plans that lead to enhanced survival. Our PFC and the home and social domains it produced began to distinguish us from all other organisms, but at an unforeseen price. As we began to recognize a future, we had to recognize that at some point we would not be part of that future—we began to recognize our own mortality.

We began to fear not only dying; we began to wonder what happens after we die. What happens to whatever it is that wonders about what happens? Does our Ic domain remain a part of a larger group, even if removed from the partnership of the biological domain? Or is it alone? Or does it exist at all? Is our Ic domain, how we see ourselves and how others see us, gone forever, whatever *it* may be? This fear of death and the unknown that follows, coupled with our human desire to be valued both during life *and* after death, contributed to some people believing in an afterlife.

Fear and God

Formalizing that afterlife created a set of rules, which, if adhered to by a group, increased the chance that you would be remembered after death. Many of these rules are fear based. "Thou shalt not . . . " is a warning: do something wrong and you run the risk of being punished and kicked out of the group. Every major religion has a set of rules and laws, but in each, the essence is to create a structure in which a person feels safer. Just thinking about death or threat changes our brain activity and increases the fear response. But thinking about religion, or some shared cultural belief, decreases that fear of death.[24] Our brains have adapted so that, in some ways, religion really is, as Karl Marx put it, the "opium of the people."[25] Marx was disdainful of religion, but, from a brain point of view, this remarkable bond among people has served a critical purpose in our evolution: it has eased the fear of mortality and encouraged us to attain a much higher ideal, one in which our actions now will be the basis of our value in the future.

Recently, a member of my community passed away after a battle with cancer. When I went to his wake, there was a line of people giving their time to recognize his passing. It took two hours to reach the casket. This man had influenced all of them, and they wanted to let his surviving wife and family know of his contribution to their lives. We truly do control no one but influence everyone, and this man chose to be a powerful influence of good.

I spoke with his best friend about the last days. He was not scared, but said poignantly that when he spoke to his God, He was very quiet. Although God was silent, this man's faith held him. This man's Ic remained recognized after his death. And as he approached death, his belief in a God was calming.

He had faith that his Ic would remain in the company of an entity so powerful that we cannot conceive it in its entirety. (In fact, a rabbi once said that if you think you understand God, then your concept of God is too small.) The calm offered by being part of a group with such a powerful protective force is compelling. Throughout history, human beings began to form different religious groups, based on a relationship in which such an afterlife image was agreed upon and shared, to which we could belong and whose rules we would adhere to, to ensure the promise of that afterlife reward. We no longer needed to only share the same village; this shared value connected us between continents.

Unfortunately, our inherent limbic fear of death can be exploited by a religion and can actually impair rational thought, our PFC. In a compelling if not disturbing study, people who listened to an evangelical preacher actually decreased blood flow to, and therefore presumed activity and function of, their PFC.[26] This is an unforeseen dark side of the release of oxytocin and being part of a group. In a religious fervor, a person can become so convinced that what they are doing has moral efficacy, and that their reward will be immortality in the afterlife, that they can enact horrific and deadly actions that include killing and maiming people believed to be threatening their group. The fear of being threatened justifies the immoral act of taking another person's life, because, through the interplay of the Ic and social domains, their Theory of Mind has become so distorted, and their biological domain has so subverted their PFC, that they can dehumanize other people and, therefore, feel no remorse or guilt in killing them.

God as One of the Greatest Media Tools Ever

On occasion in a therapy session, something will pop into my head that I intend to say out loud. I alert my patient to an upcoming idea with phrases like, "This may seem like it is coming from left field," or, "Remember how I told you I may say things you don't want to hear but I'm going to say them anyway? Well here comes one of those," or "Warning, I am about to get shrinky."

Well what I am about to talk about is one of those things, and it may really get some people angry. It has to do with how I believe that religion is one of the best marketing campaigns ever, often relying on fear to bind people to a moral ethic. The remarkably cynical view is that God has been used as a means of scaring people into being good, moral, ethical people who follow rules and try very hard not to hurt anyone else. The fear of going to an eternal damnation later promotes being good now.

But a deeper utility of religion is the promise of an afterlife, and that promise would not be necessary if human beings did not have a concept of time—and a concept of a limited amount of time we call "life." From this point of view, religion becomes a way to decrease the terror we have of our own mortality, by giving us a sense of immortality, protection, meaning, and purpose if we follow a religion and its teachings. In fact, a group out of the University of Missouri–Columbia wrote a paper about this in 2009 entitled "A Terror Management Analysis of the Psychological Functions of Religion."[27] Religion creates a "psychological security and hope of immortality."[28]

Our fear of death can only come about by having self-awareness, an Ic domain that provides an insight into who we are, awareness of our mortality and that we are not going to be here forever. I am not smart enough to know if there is or is not a God, although I believe in some higher power. But I am fairly sure that for those who believe, it is remarkably comforting to be part of a group where there is such a powerful protector. Who wouldn't adhere to whatever rules may be required to remain of value in that social domain? Let me take a moment of personal privilege and say I look forward to the day when our collective PFC can recognize that all these gods are the same, just with a different name. We are one group, sharing the boons and foibles of being a social animal.

Moving to a Different I-M

Just as in the chapter on the home domain, this is not about blaming the media for the fear generated in the social domain. The people in media are also at their I-M. The spirit of the media is to impart knowledge to the populace, alerting them to the dangers lurking behind the rustle of the bush. No doubt there is enormous survival benefit to knowing what the dangers are outside the confines of your home. And for that, the media deserve thanks. But the media have also exploited our deep desire as social animals to be valued by other human beings and gain membership to the group, and the equally deep fear of being seen with less value and at risk of being kicked out of the group. Exploiting our brain, which automatically compares sets of information, the media suggest we do just that: compare ourselves to the rest of our society. Will my coworker get the job because he has more value than I do? Will the boy I like choose someone with more value than me? Will the college choose someone more valuable than me? Will the other race, the other religion, the other country prevail because they have more value than mine? This comparison is the source of a lot of fear.

But I am convinced there is more to the world than a predator or marauder waiting to strike. Rather than seeing the world as a place of divisive groups, the I-M Approach suggests that there is actually no limit to the size of the group. Each of us has an I-M, each of us has evolved basically the same brain, and each of us simply wants to feel as if we are a valued member of the group.

————————— Exercise —————————

PUTTING IT ALL TOGETHER

Your I-M is influenced by the four domains of biological, Ic, home, and social. Before we go to the last chapter, take a moment to reflect on how these four domains have influenced your fear and the fears of those in your inner circle. You may want to take the I-M graph and jot down some notes next to each of the domains.

FIGURE 4

The I-M Approach

What happened at home? How did that influence your choices in the social domain of career, relationships, place to live, etc.? How have these two external domains influenced your Ic—how you see yourself and how you think others see you? How is your self-esteem, and how do other people see you? Some of the most productive people I know still have self-doubt. How about you? And how has this impression influenced the biological domain of your brain and body? If you do have stress, anxiety, or any medical condition, how does this influence your choices in the three other domains? I recommend you are fearless in your assessment, honest, and *respect*ful. When fearless, you do not activate the limbic reflex to run—in this case, run from who you are. Instead, put your hand on your forehead and kick in that PFC. There is nothing to run from, no saber-toothed tiger lurking in your unconscious. This is how you can really begin to change to a different I-M, by assessing the one you are at, at this particular moment in time. But I invite you to come back to this exercise often. You may be amazed at how your I-M changes, even on a daily basis!

I-M Moving Forward

As long as we continue to view ourselves as lacking, as long as we compare ourselves as we are to how we think we should be, we are always at risk of being ruled by fear. In the home domain chapter, I spoke about Fabian who had worried he would disappoint his parents. Once they realized the pressure he felt, they were able to help him move to a different I-M so he could pursue his academic career. Fear can be replaced with curiosity. Because curiosity itself is squelched by fear, hence the saying "curiosity killed the cat," using the I-M Approach encourages looking again at why that person is doing what he or she is doing, without the moral overlay of judgment. And this is exactly what the I-M offers for you: looking at your fear without judgment but with wonder and curiosity, two functions of your PFC.

The I-M Approach helps us do this on a global level, not just one individual at a time, but one entire country, race, or religion at a time. If every individual is at an I-M, then so is the group in which that individual finds membership. And as we will explore in the next chapter, there is no limit to the size of the group. We are in this together, and how we influence each other's Ic domain has an enormous impact on how we overcome our fear reflex.

5

Traversing
Together

Piglet sidled up to Pooh from behind. "Pooh?" he whispered.
"Yes, Piglet?"
"Nothing," said Piglet, taking Pooh's hand.
"I just wanted to be sure of you."
—A.A. Milne, *Winnie-the-Pooh*

Peter had been an anxious child, an anxious teenager, and was now an anxious adult. When he was in his early 30s, he came into my office after being discharged from yet another rehab, struggling with his addiction to prescription medicine. He did not want to use, but he had found so little relief from the relentless torture of high-level anxiety, always on alert, always in fear. In his heart of hearts, he wanted to be sober. But addiction does not happen in the heart, it happens in the brain. He was already on nonaddictive medication for anxiety and had been doing basic cognitive-behavioral therapy, but he was still scared of being home, scared of going to work, scared of relapsing. Together we were about to embark on an exploration of the four domains that was his journey to his I-M, recognizing that at each step he was at a current maximum potential.

One of the questions I asked Peter, and ask all my patients, is to tell me, without editing, the first memory that comes to mind. This limbic memory is often a clue as to the source of the fear. Peter told me a memory of other kids running away from him in his neighborhood. When kids saw him coming, they would duck and hide from him, but only after they were sure that he knew they had seen him approaching. These were children's brains (the biological I-M of a brain where the PFC is less developed than the limbic system), wanting to feel pleasure, take risks, and be social. They were also impulsive and emotional, not able to fully anticipate the future. There was no reason for them to be so cruel, but they formed a group, risked getting in trouble from a protective adult, and found pleasure by ostracizing Peter and bonding closer with a common goal. Ditching Peter was never intended to be crippling. They just thought they were having fun. Peter also had a limbic brain, with a developing Ic and an intact Theory of Mind. Peter was beginning to see himself as an outcast, with very little value.

All these years later in my office, Peter's biological domain filled his brain and body with cortisol and adrenaline, just thinking about being around them, being teased by them, being reminded over and over that he was not cool enough to be part of their group.

He wanted to end the session right then and go home. Home was a source of comfort, of safety, but Peter began to realize that he had also seen home as a place to escape, which, in retrospect, he realized meant he did not see himself as capable enough to manage his fear outside the protective walls of his house. His Ic domain, he realized all these years later as an adult sitting in the safety of my office, had been beaten down so much that he believed he was as worthless as he thought the other kids saw him to be.

But he stayed and went on with his story.

Sometime around seventh grade, another kid, a popular kid, took pity on Peter. This popular kid took Peter under his wing, escorted him into the woods with the other kids, and got him stoned. The first time Peter smoked, nothing much happened. He was just so happy to be part of the cool kid group. He couldn't know that his brain was being primed, and was responding to the change in the biological domain the best the brain could. But the next time his new friend took him into the woods to get high, Peter accepted the joint that was passed to him and took a tentative drag. The next time the joint came around his way he took a deeper puff, coughing as the smoke filled his lungs. But then another feeling overcame him. He was high. He was basking in a calm that felt really, really good. For the first time in as long as he could remember, he felt something other than fear.

His brain became conditioned very quickly. Peter began to associate drugs with calm. But every time he used a drug to relieve his anxiety, he unwittingly convinced himself that he was not able to deal with the very fear he was trying to avoid. So the next time he began to feel fear, his brain would go, "Hey. You know what to do. Get high!" In this way, he began to increase the very thing he was trying to overcome. For if you do not think you are strong enough to deal with something, what do you think happens to your anxiety? It sure doesn't get less; in fact, it just gets worse. Peter was training his brain to think that he was not able to deal with his fear without drugs.

But now, two decades later, he sat across from me telling me the most remarkable story. Peter was in a relationship with a woman who had a teenage son who also struggled with anxiety. Peter saw in himself an opportunity to be of help. He could be valuable to the boy. And the fact that he had a girlfriend meant that, through her eyes, he was also worthy of a relationship and of being loved.

The three of them had gone for a walk on a beach in the middle of a very cold and snowy winter. The day before, an enormous nor'easter had blanketed New England with a thick coating of deep, dense snow. The three were leaving their footprints behind them on the snow-covered beach. Peter and the teenager began to walk farther down the shore, out toward the ocean, while the boy's mom began to fall farther behind, her face reddened by the cold but feeling happy that her son and her boyfriend were developing a relationship.

Peter and the boy kept trudging, amazed at how far out the tide had gone. They kept walking through the ever-thinning layer of snow, then turned and waved back to the woman waiting about one hundred feet behind. And then Peter heard a slight crack. Then another, and another—and then he realized with a burst of cortisol and adrenaline that they were not on the sands at all but on a layer of ice. The ocean had frozen, and they had walked about one hundred feet on the ice-cold waters of the Atlantic.

The sound of ice cracking began to fill Peter's senses, and that old familiar fear began to take over. He wanted to run, to get away, feeling the same fear as when he had been teased and persecuted in his childhood. He recognized this I-M of fear, but did not like it, nor condone it, and quickly held himself responsible for it by respecting that this was part of his history—but it didn't have to be part of his next current maximum potential.

The boy was a few feet ahead of him. As Peter's I-M shifted, he shouted to the boy to turn back. And as he did, the boy, his arms suddenly pulled into the air as if by a puppet string, gave a yelp and was gone, sucked into the sea.

The head and arms of the boy bobbed up again. Peter began to rush toward the boy as the ice cracked beneath him, and then he was also under. He dragged himself out onto the ice, it broke again, and the boy began to dip beneath his field of vision. Peter gave one enormous lunge and, in a fluid motion, lurched out of the ice-cold ocean and spread his shivering body flat on the ice, distributing his weight on the fragile surface. His arm reached out to the boy, and praying to a higher power that the ice would hold, he grabbed the boy by an outstretched hand.

"Climb over me!" he told the boy, who sputtered with a mouth full of seawater, panicking as he thought he was going to die. "I've got you. I've got you. Climb over me." Peter held on, giving the boy the support he needed to use Peter's body as a brace and ladder to clamber out of the relentless sea.

As Peter became a plank of stability, he felt the boy moving over his body. The two turned slowly, methodically, like the arms of a clock, toward the beach. There, frantic, with a crowd beginning to form around her, was the boy's mother, terrified she would lose two loved ones in one wave. Peter and the boy began to slide themselves across the ice toward a shore of solid ground.

Peter sat in my office, his body trembling as he told me the story. He had been extremely afraid, but had not let his fear overcome him. We spoke about this amazing metaphor. For most of his life, his I-M had been traversing on thin ice, always afraid, waiting to fall into the abyss of his anxiety that would consume him like the waves of an ocean. And yet, in this real moment of very real danger, he had not succumbed. He had, instead, saved a life. He did not turn and run to save himself; he faced the danger, gave of himself to that teenager, and to his girlfriend who watched in horror from the shore. Peter had reached an entirely different I-M in the moment between hearing the first crack of the ice and watching the boy disappear. He had overcome his fear and become a hero, a benefactor.

As this realization swept over him, his trembling stopped. His eyes widened not in fear but in astonishment as the profundity of the experience began to burrow into his Ic domain. He had been on thin ice, but now he was on solid ground, back on shore where he had received a warm and passionate hug from his girlfriend, a firm and grateful embrace from the boy, and the cheers and hoorays from a crowd of strangers who had watched the event unfold. One had called an ambulance, and as the EMTs wrapped warm blankets around the two survivors, Peter felt a radiance of safety and security he said he had never felt before. This was not from the blanket that covered his shoulders, but from somewhere deep inside.

He was valuable, he was capable, he was able to overcome his fear.

But it was not just that Peter saw himself in this way—so did all those other people. It was through the eyes of others that Peter's I-M had really changed, starting with developing an attachment to his girlfriend and her son that led them to the walk on the beach. We really do control no one but influence everyone.

Let's go back to each of the four domains and see how the application of the I-M Approach creates a simple, practical, and easily applied method to reduce our own fear and the fear of others in our biological, home, Ic, and social domains.

Traversing Together in the Biological Domain

I've said this already but it bears repeating; it's something I have learned in my field about the way our brains work that may seem obvious to some people, but for some reason, it's not to everyone. *People prefer pleasure over pain, and not just that—we are hardwired to create pleasure over pain.*

The unique pleasure and reward of being part of a group gets reinforced through the effect of oxytocin, the "cuddle" hormone. In case you forgot, oxytocin is the neurohormone I brought up earlier. I'm bringing it up again here because oxytocin is that human glue that connects us in a virtual and very real way—we just can't talk about reducing fear without talking about increasing oxytocin.

We can elicit the release of oxytocin in another person, and other people can elicit the release of oxytocin in us. When I stroke my youngster's hair or give my older son a hug, I am helping his brain release oxytocin. When my wife gives me a supportive hug, she is increasing oxytocin in me. This is something all of us do with other people as well, and not just family members. Peter did this for the boy he saved and his mother, and they reciprocated. And all the others—most of whom were total strangers—did this for Peter. We have known about the healing and calming properties of this molecule for more than fifty years. A meta-analysis of 102 studies of oxytocin between 1959 and 2010 was published recently in the *Journal of Affective Disorders*. The authors found that oxytocin reliably induced "a general sense of well-being including calm, improved social interactions, increased trust, and reduced fear."[1] Oxytocin reduces blood pressure, increases a desire to be with other people, and makes social interactions feel rewarding.

Even the simplest acts of kindness and caring can influence our biological domain to make and release oxytocin—a supportive touch of the hand, a pat on the back, believing that someone else understands what you are going through and cares.

A great example of this occurred in a teenage group I was facilitating. Sarah was sitting next to Anita in group therapy one day as she quietly described the experiences of being molested and abused by a relative as an adolescent. She began to cry, the fear and vulnerability palpable to everyone in the room. Anita touched the crying girl's arm in a gesture of support. The effect was striking, as an entire room of teenagers—boys and girls, kids from good homes and broken homes, kids with psychiatric conditions, kids detoxing from drugs and alcohol—were attentive. They offered words of support, showing their confidence that Sarah was not to blame, was a good person, and was a valuable member of the group. Her tears did not stop, but she was able to keep talking and share her secrets without fear of being judged. As a result of Sarah sharing her fears and traumas and the supportive reaction of the group, everyone reached a different I-M that day.

Anita and others in the group recognized Sarah's fear and her deep-seated feelings of inadequacy as a result of her trauma, and each member of the group responded in the most compassionate and intelligent way he or she could. When you can recognize fear in others and embrace it through respect and discussion, you can reduce that fear, and everyone involved will have their feelings addressed and respected.

In other words, your brain has an influence on someone else's brain. Traversing together, we can reduce the fear in another person and help her feel calm, collected, and *connected*. We can replace fear with trust.

One of the things you start to learn in my business, especially when you've been in the field for many years, is that our intuition and experience is sometimes decades ahead of hard science. But the good news now is that science can finally back up what we've felt and observed for a long time—that these simple warm touches and expressions of support have calming and healing effects on people.

A group at Brigham Young University in Utah invited thirty-four married couples to participate in a study investigating the healing and stress-reducing properties of oxytocin. They measured both their cortisol and oxytocin levels over a four-week period. The couples were asked to do just one intervention: offer a warm touch as a way to connect with their partners when talking with each other. They were taught to simply reach out and perhaps touch their partner's hand or shoulder, or massage their neck to relieve stress. This small change had a big effect, influencing the biological domain of the other person—oxytocin increased and cortisol levels lowered, suggesting to the researchers that, in fact, the warm touch relieved the other person's stress. One of the most startling findings was that the husbands in particular had lower blood pressure than those who were not given a hug by their wives.[2] If oxytocin is secreted as a result of human

▶ UNFROZEN IN THE ELEVATOR

Four-year-old Kaelyn Kerr was on her way to a hair salon with her mom and little brother when suddenly the elevator they were in stopped and got stuck, trapping them inside. When the Reading, Massachusetts, fire department arrived, they found the only way to get the family out was through the hatch in the ceiling of the elevator. They had to lower a ladder into the car to help the family get out. Little Kaelyn, frozen by fear, couldn't climb the ladder.

But some of the rescue workers had young children themselves and thought they'd try something to help her relax her fears. They started singing a popular song that everyone, even some big, burly firefighters, knew: the popular hit, so aptly named for this occasion, "Let it Go," from the Disney movie *Frozen*. Kaelyn had seen the movie many times, as had the firefighters' kids. One of the rescuers, Scott Myette, told NBC News, "I'm slightly embarrassed to admit this, but yeah, I pretty much knew all of [the words]. It's not a bad song, it just gets stuck in your head a bit."

Kaelyn's mom found it pretty hilarious that these two grown men knew the entire ballad, but was grateful they were able to figure out a solution. In fact, Kaelyn was so calmed that she even wanted to go back to the salon for her hair appointment.

To my mind, there is probably no clearer example of traversing together (to trust) than what happened in this true story. The only thing that is odd about it is that it is viewed as a sweet "news" story, as if it doesn't happen a lot. I would argue that it does happen a lot, but could certainly happen a lot more if these incidents could be reported more often instead of the fear-inducing stories that are so prevalent.[3]

interaction, then we do indeed have a powerful effect on each other's state of mind, and that includes our more challenging mental states like fear, stress, and anger.

Using your knowledge of how fear works in yourself and in your different domains, you can influence other people's fears and improve their I-Ms. And by the way, that's not just being altruistic. It's improving your own I-M, strengthening all of our domains against fears, and calming everyone down.

One of the things I teach my psychiatry students is that "intuition is the precursor to technique." We all have intuitive responses to each other, in essence limbic ancient reflexive ways of interacting. If you rudely interrupt me in conversation, my reflex is to become angry. If you help me when my groceries fall, my reflex is to be relaxed and want to repay you in some way. This is usually how people feel reflexively, and they react accordingly. Sometimes our reflex response isn't productive, though, and this inhibits our I-M. This can often happen when someone else is dealing with a fear reflex and you're in the vicinity. Think of the drowning person who will grab on to you, pulling you down too. He can't help it—that's his I-M at that point in time.

When people are afraid, they often behave reflexively in ways that bring out other peoples' worst reflexes. Many of the rescue workers who tried to rescue the family from the elevator could have just started yelling at the little girl, to try to force her to climb the ladder. It's possible that thought occurred to one of them. "Just get that kid on the ladder and haul her up" could have been a very natural thought in that moment. But the firefighters used their intuition, then reflected. The experience of having young children helped them develop their intuition, but we all have it and need to listen to it more often.

When we're reflecting, we're using our PFC; when we're in reflexive mode, we're stuck in the limbo of our limbic system. You have the choice: you can listen to your intuition and reflect.

Traversing Together in the Ic Domain

The Ic domain is powerful. It is through this domain and Theory of Mind that our home and social domains exert their positive influence, which results in the biological domain's increase or decrease of oxytocin. When Amanda, who had the paralyzed arm, saw her little girl reach out to her, she responded. It was not just that Amanda saw *herself* as a good mother; it was that Amanda realized that *her little girl* saw her as a needed, valuable source of comfort. That was what released Amanda from her fear and paralysis—her daughter saw her at an I-M as doing the best she could, and wanted more!

Think about this for a minute: How do you react to other people you know who buy self-help books? For some reason, many people think that someone who buys these books must have something wrong with her, and is perhaps even festering with serious problems. Because that person might have "flaws" (that you couldn't possibly have!), you might respect her less, which is likely to influence your relationship with her.

We are very reluctant to look at our flaws because, if flawed, we may lose our value to others and be rejected. This fear has inhibited us for millennia, robbing us of daring to be creative, of daring to take a risk for fear of looking stupid, daring to apply for a new job, talk to that person we're attracted to, or start a business. The I-M Approach reminds us that all of those thoughts we have about our flaws are limbic reactions, not PFC reflections.

All too often I hear patients say they are afraid of therapy, of digging too deep and breaking down the walls of resistance, because they are not sure they will like what they find. But even more, they fear they will find flaws that make others perceive them with less value as a human being.

The I-M Approach allows us to forget about all that. That fear is your current maximum potential. But when you apply the I-M Approach, you can look without judgment at why you do what you do. When you do not fear what you may discover, you need not succumb to that fear and run or freeze. This is critical to understand, especially in the Ic domain, because once you can engage in I-M thinking for yourself, you can do it for others. You can stop judging yourself and acknowledge instead that you are at an I-M that can change at any moment. Then, you can bring this approach into all the other domains of your life. Realizing we are all really at an I-M, we can approach our fear with a much more productive option: trust.

Trusting yourself helps you trust others and reduces your own fears in all the domains.

Traversing Together in the Home Domain

You might think that traversing together to trust in the home domain is a "no-brainer." Of all the people in the world, whom could you trust more than your family? But learning to take the I-M Approach in the home domain can be such a valuable tool because trust goes far beyond the idea of someone's infidelity or a teenager stealing the silver to sell for drugs. Of course those things do involve trust, but there's much more.

As a child psychiatrist, I have had the opportunity to see how the I-M Approach and trust work together in the home domain quite frequently. I've seen the healing power of parents who begin to recognize that their kid is at an I-M, and instead of judging him harshly, feeling disappointed, they begin to wonder why he is doing what he is doing. You have probably seen this too but may not have recognized it.

Think back to the story of Fabian in chapter 3, where we left him smoking marijuana, struggling in school—"being lazy" is what his parents thought, as he became more and more estranged from them. But then Fabian and his parents began to use the I-M Approach, looking at the influence of the four domains not just on Fabian's academics, but on his parents' sense of fear and desperation for their son. It was only when his parents shifted their perspective of Fabian's efforts, from one of thinking he was lazy to one of appreciation of his I-M, that he began to excel in his academics.

Fabian was also willing to look at how his parents were at an I-M themselves. He realized that their different expectations of each other had resulted in a family I-M that was tense and hostile, one rife with disappointments. His parents were willing to look at how they may have scared him by placing too many demands on him, even as they thought they were communicating confidence that Fabian could manage. Their son, not wanting to disappoint, began to feel inadequate, fearful that his parents would be angry and see him as "less than."

Fabian's parents began to appreciate the coalescence of these pressures and were able to express to him that they were only worried, that they thought he was amazing, and that they always saw him as the most valuable person in the world. While this might all seem a bit sentimental to the cynics out there, it's important to remember that many of us go through our days with negative dialogues going on in our heads. But in the instant when we hear the truth from the so-called "horse's mouth"—whether it be from a parent, a child, or other close relative—we feel a surge in value. I know that I, as a psychiatrist, feel a surge of value when I can see how the I-M Approach works to bring people together.

Fabian was perhaps no different from most teenagers who are at times confused, depressed, angry, and certainly, anxious. They can easily drift into alcohol and other drugs because of these pressures. So it's especially important for parents to help alleviate the pressures and fears of their teens and rekindle their sense of value, encourage interests, and help broaden their imagination so that fear doesn't move into it.

—————————— Exercise ——————————

WHISPERS AND WINKS

In Chapter 3, "Unexpected Undercurrents," we explored the subtle fears that can stem from our home domain. Take a moment to think about a few things that you are afraid of now, and which of those may have been, or still are, influenced by your home domain. Spiders? Dentists? People with dark skin or different religious beliefs or from different cultures? How about people with psychiatric conditions or addictions? Was there a family member your parents talked about in whispers—maybe it was that uncle they wondered if they should invite to a wedding because nobody was comfortable with him?

While some of these things may have warranted fear as a little kid, you are older now, have experienced more of life, are more capable, and are learning that everyone, everyone, is at an I-M. How do you turn your home into one in which trust is not confined just to those who do and say what they are expected to?

You can you begin by practicing and teaching your kids about the I-M Approach, and show them through your actions that everyone in their home and social domains is at a current maximum potential. Don't be afraid to try.

——————————————————————————

Traversing Together in the Social Domain:
Using the I-M Approach to Put It All Together

Remember Tracy from the last chapter, the woman so crippled by a social anxiety that it manifested into agoraphobic panic attacks? To Tracy, the social domain was one of terror. It was only in the safer confines of my office that she learned how to use the I-M Approach and began to question why the best she could do was to remain an emotional cripple, trapped by her fears. She didn't like her current I-M and desperately wanted, needed, to change it.

In therapy, Tracy recalled her earliest memories and the very strong attachment she had to her father. He doted on her, told her she was the most beautiful thing in the world, and treated her as a fragile flower. It was his way of showing he valued her. In large part, this is the only way she knew how to be valued, as she hadn't been as close to her mother and her older brother, who was a bit of a bully and who appeared jealous over what he perceived as preferential treatment.

It was when Tracy was in her mid-twenties, after her father passed away, that her fear kicked into gear. She felt alone now, with nobody to back her up emotionally the way her father had. How was she meant to survive in the world without his protection? And her brother didn't help at all. Instead, he berated her for her neediness, for being such a daddy's girl, and told her that it was time for her to grow up. He saw her as spoiled and inadequate, and with no dad there to buffer that influence on her Ic domain, she shriveled emotionally. She withdrew into the safety of her home—but that very safety became her prison.

Tracy didn't like her fear, didn't condone her fear, and began to hold herself responsible for her fear so that she was able to respect her fear: re = again, spect = look. Fear held power over her and deserved to be confronted. At first, Tracy thought this was the stupidest thing ever. How could her fear be the best she could do? Even this resistance was an I-M, but as Tracy continued to remain crippled by her anxiety, she used her PFC to try something different: she gave the I-M Approach a chance.

Gradually Tracy moved from reflexive and limbic to reflective and prefrontal. It wasn't immediate, but before long—in the social domain of my office, where she was not rejected, was not going to be cast out, and was not afraid—she had an epiphany: *the people in the mall, on the street, or in the grocery store were not her brother.* In fact, they had the potential to be just as kind as her dad. She thought of her dad and how much he had valued her. His view of her as a delicate flower was not the same as seeing her as weak and unable to care for herself. Instead, his view of her was as someone truly special, someone worthy of enormous value, not of deriding rejection as from her jealous brother. In fact, she recognized how strong she was to withstand her brother's relentless bullying. Even if it had eroded her self-esteem as a child, she did not need to succumb to his anger anymore. She may not be perfect, but she was doing the best she could.

———————— Exercise ————————

HOW TO BE A FEAR FIGHTER

Jorge was an eleven-year-old I treated for anxiety. In a session one time, he told me that one of the greatest recent moments of his life—his *life*—was when another kid chose him for a capture the flag game at recess. On a daily basis, human beings worry about whether we will fit into a group, and we experience enormous relief when we fit in. Jorge felt so good to be part of a team, to be included with a bunch of other kids running around, that he completely forgot his anxiety.

Being chosen for a team was just one small thing, but it meant being included, something huge for Jorge, and it significantly impacted his brain. The captain of the team became a good friend, and more friends followed. Jorge would still get worried when heading over to play with one of his new friends, but he recognized this was his I-M and did not let it interfere with the potential fun he was going to have.

Think about this story the next time you find yourself in a position to help another person. When you do some small thing for someone else, you become a benefactor. Benefactors are highly prized and valued in a group, as they help increase the chances that other group members will survive and thrive. By enhancing your own value to the group you decrease your anxiety and fear, the fear of being cast out of that protective group.

Although all of Tracy's imperfections remained, they no longer had to reduce her to a life of isolation, unless that is what she *chose* for an I-M. And she didn't. Her Ic domain began to shift. A vision of herself as valuable, without a need to be "perfect," emerged. Tracy still would feel anxious as she drove to the mall, but she was able to reflect on this reflex and use her PFC to analyze the problem, come up with a solution, keep driving, and anticipate that there was really no need to be stifled, frozen, and afraid. No one was really assessing her with a critical eye, intent on humiliating her or having her kicked out of some group.

On the contrary, she might even meet someone new when she got a new job or when she went to the mall or library. This was a different I-M. Tracy was able to leave the prison of her home and venture out into more and more social domains. She began to recognize other people's I-Ms and other people's fears. This strengthened her confidence and further diminished her fear. She was now able to enjoy the freedom of creativity and exploration offered by her new I-M.

The Choice to Heal: Trust over Fear

From my experience as a psychiatrist, there is no question in my mind that part of the healing process in my patients is a result of what is called a "psychotherapeutic attachment."[4] Early experiences in relationships have an influence on brain development, likely laying down neural pathways between the PFC and limbic system that influence the responses of our Ic and biological domains to the home and social environments.

Over time, these pathways become like highways, directing

our interpretation of perceived situations and creating patterns of response. These responses form the foundation of our relationships in the future, not always the most productive, but at an I-M. The home domain influences the choices we make in the social domain and the relationships and attachments we make with other people. In psychotherapy, these patterns can be explored from the respect, value, and trust of the therapeutic alliance the counselor and patient form; patients can examine the choices they make using their PFC, and new choices can evolve, leading to more productive relationships.

But I do not think the healing relationship for these changes need be confined to the therapist's office. Although most of us are not trained therapists, each of us has basically the same brain, interested in what other people think or feel about us. As such, each of us has the ability to induce fear or trust in others. Without real intention, we do this to each other all the time, just as Amanda's mother at first empowered her daughter's sense of value, and then devalued her daughter by worrying she would drop the baby. Or as Tracy's dad did by treating her as fragile, even as she was toughened up by her bullying brother.

We may not always be aware of the influence we have on each other, innocently inducing fear or trust in another person as effortlessly and thoughtlessly as breathing. And yet, if we were indeed to think about it, to shift from an impulsive limbic brain to a more controlled and thoughtful one, my guess is that each of us would rather have someone trust us than fear us, just as we would rather trust than fear.

Trust brings with it the promise of an alliance. Fear brings with it the potential of that person retreating and leaving us alone and vulnerable, or retaliating with anger and approaching us with the intention of making us afraid instead. The first is much more pleasurable. If the brain is going to choose between fear and pleasure, it will choose pleasure every time. But perhaps we have been limbic for so long we thwart the very hedonic experience we so avidly seek, inhibited instead by fear.

The Challenge to the I-M Approach

All of the stories I've included in this book involve people who were going through challenges in their lives; we're no different from them because, if you're alive, you're going to face challenges. Sometimes we're in better places than others. When we begin to see ourselves as doing the best we can, we can forgive ourselves and respect ourselves a bit more, even if we don't like or condone what we do. It is easier to hold ourselves responsible and accountable because we can do so without judgment. Instead, we can begin to move off the thin ice of fear and self-doubt on which we travel, and move onto the solid ground of a new shore of trust and self-respect.

But the real power comes in when we begin to recognize that *everyone* is at an I-M. Everyone is simply at a current maximum potential, doing the best they can, given the influence of the four domains in their lives. When we do this, we can approach people with wonder rather than worry, with interest rather than mistrust. The acceptance this communicates has a very different influence in their Ic domain than if we approach them with the message that they should be doing better, that they are not respected or valued, and may not have a place in our group. The I-M Approach changes all that, and very quickly.

Perhaps the hardest thing to accept when applying the I-M Approach is that even people who commit crimes, or are racist or intolerant—people with whom you would never want to hang out—even they are at their I-M. We hold these people accountable, but we can still approach them with respect and avoid setting ourselves up as their judge, deciding who is doing the best they can and who isn't. Judgment breeds fear and can only perpetuate someone's sense of being isolated and alone, which will in turn perpetuate more of the anger and fear that leads people to commit crimes in the first place.

─────────── Exercise ───────────

CAN YOU READ MINDS?

The next time you expose yourself to media, whether newspaper, Web, or TV reports, check in using the I-M Approach. Say you read a horrific tragedy involving someone with a lot of personal problems. Your limbic system immediately goes on alert and is likely to have a reflexive response to what you are exposed to. But then put the palm of your hand on your forehead like a mind reader, and get that PFC going. Reflect for a moment on the back story of the people you are reading about.

What was their home domain like? How did this influence their choices in the social domain? While you may never know for sure, the exercise helps give you perspective on the black-and-white approach of media reports. Life is full of gray areas, especially when it comes to human beings. This is why it's helpful to practice applying the I-M Approach to daily life. We may not like nor condone a person's current maximum potential; that person is held responsible for her I-M, but you can respect her I-M as the best she can do at that moment in time.

─────────────────────────────

In my field of psychiatry, I often see the tendency to ostracize and alienate people who are struggling. Human beings can be incredibly cruel, quick to judge, and quick to dismiss. This is all too often the reflexive response to my patients with psychiatric conditions and addictions: Get them out of my neighborhood. They aren't like me. They should be doing better. What's wrong with them? I believe that these are the very people who need a protective group—who need *us* the most.

I have seen this approach work repeatedly with my adolescents struggling with addiction. Many of them are using because they already feel so ostracized, and the only pleasure they can experience is through mood-altering chemicals. But the problem is, the more they use, the more they distance themselves from the very people who are trying to connect with them. I see it happen regularly that within just a few days of being treated with respect in the course of using the I-M Approach (and activating their Ic domain through ToM and their oxytocin in their biological domain!) they begin to feel more valuable. I am routinely astonished by the resilience of these kids when they know their I-M, whatever it is at a given time, is *recognized* and *respected*. The path to their sobriety is through us—by traversing together we can rekindle their sense of value and allow them to trust.

By making the decision to see people at their I-M, you not only reduce their fear and increase their sense of safety and value; *you* also become less afraid and feel the safety of being a valuable contributing member of the group. When you help another person feel valuable, you enhance your own Ic, as a *benefactor*—a position of great value in the social domain.

Passing Down the I-M Approach

You probably know something about the basics of genetics, that we inherit traits from our parents: eye color, cheekbones, dimples, both external and internal manifestations that result when our mom's genes combine with our dad's. Sometimes these genes mutate, sometimes they rearrange. It has been only via these mechanisms that inheritance and evolution were thought to occur. If you got a "good" set of genes from your parents, you were more likely to survive and pass those genes on to the next generation.[5] But as we learn more and more about genetics, we've also learned from scientists in a field called "epigenetics," how our environment can really influence our genes, turning them on and off, and how these genetic switches can be passed on to the next generation and the next.

When it comes to fear, knowing your genetics can be helpful, but it can also be helpful to know what has happened in recent history to your ancestors. I talk about epigenetics to the kids I work with who may be struggling with fears and anxieties that they are self-medicating or numbing with alcohol and other drugs. Some of these kids may have come from violent families in the past, or from war-torn countries, or populations persecuted in recent generations. There is significant data showing how powerful the environment is, not only in altering people's psychology, but their actual genetic tags. And these can be passed on, with possible increased risks, to their offspring.

I am not trying to scare the kids when I share this knowledge, but instead trying to encourage and empower them. The reality is that no one will ever be scared out of using drugs. If the brain is going to choose between fear and pleasure, it will choose pleasure every time. But there is also pleasure in power and knowledge is power. The knowledge to understand addiction gives them the power to make choices and hopefully the recognition that we control no one but influence everyone. So in a very real way, *we* are the epigenetic forces on each other.

The I-M blends two powerful external domains of home and social worlds with the two internal domains of our self-concept and our biology. The result is our I-M, our current maximum potential. It is another way for these kids who are self-medicating their fear with drugs to appreciate the genetic and now epigenetic forces and how addiction and sobriety play their parts. It is a way to understand how fear can enter into our lives—or sadness, or anger, or love, or happiness, or any of the myriad responses we have to the opportunities we experience.

The I-M Approach serves as a road map to explore, safely and without judgment, why we do what we do. When we start to look at ourselves and others this way, it may be a small change but can have a big effect. And when we see others at an I-M, we can have an influence on their biological domain and their brains through the Ic domain. We are in this together, as part of someone's home or social domain, and you get to choose what kind of influence you want to be on someone else's I-M. What kind of influence do you want to be?

I like acronyms. Take a moment to check out the acronym that emerges from the chapter titles:

Tiny	**T**errors
Rapid	**R**esponse
Unexpected	**U**ndercurrents
Social	**S**ecurity
Traversing	**T**ogether

As you can see now, the antidote to fear is as simple as trust, and the enactment of trust is faith. When I trust you, I have faith that you are not going to try to kick me out of the group. Instead, that trust is a safe foundation from which I can traverse the world and my own creative process. The I-M Approach presents the opportunity for all of us to do just that. Respect leads to value. Value leads to trust. And trust allows us to explore and express our unlimited human potential—the daring that has led to discoveries that have changed our world, like harnessing fire and creating the wheel, the printing press, refrigeration, medicines, and many more. But beyond these inventions, trust leads to two PFC brains traversing together, working, playing, forming relationships, and having faith, just like the people in the stories in this book.

Hearing the Music

What happens when we respond to the fear reflex by seeing ourselves as at an I-M, as doing the best we can?

- We recognize we are not powerless
- We forgive ourselves
- We see that we are more in control of our lives than we thought
- We can look at the influences on our I-M as a guide to understanding why we do what we do
- We can begin to move toward how we want to be seen, and how we want to see ourselves
- We begin to respect ourselves, and can then make choices on how we want to treat ourselves
- We can own, take responsibility for, and respect our current I-M
- We can see other people that way as well
- We realize that we control no one but influence everyone

There is a cartoon by Gary Larson where a chubby boy with glasses is playing a tuba behind an outhouse. In the distance stands a small crowd of people looking in the direction of the outhouse, and it's clear they don't see the boy and think the boy's music is what you'd expect to hear coming out of an outhouse.

This book asks you to look beyond the outhouse.

When we receive a message that we are not good enough, we fear. When we send a message that the other person is not good enough, we create fear. And when that other person responds the way a fearful brain has evolved to respond, he runs away, and we are left alone, undefended from the very predators we formed social groups to protect ourselves from to begin with. But more, just like those people with their vision blocked by the outhouse, we will miss our own and each other's music.

When we truly see ourselves and everyone around us as re-markable human beings, doing the best we can with what we know at this given time, fear loses its power. We can trust that we have value to the people in this vast group called "humanity," and we can see and affirm their value.

We can then say with confidence and with hope for what we can become:

We are all I-M.

Notes

Chapter 1: Tiny Terrors

1. D. J. Linden, *The Accidental Mind: How Brain Evolution Has Given Us Love, Memory, Dreams, and God* (Cambridge, MA: Harvard University Press, 2007).

2. J. H. de Groot, G. R. Semin, and M. A. Smeets, "I Can See, Hear, and Smell Your Fear: Comparing Olfactory and Audiovisual Media in Fear Communication," *Journal of Experimental Psychology General* 143, no. 2 (April 2014): 825–34, doi:10.1037/a0033731, e-pub, July 15, 2013.

3. D. Chen, A. Katdare, and N. Lucas, "Chemosignals of Fear Enhance Cognitive Performance in Humans," *Chemical Senses* 31, no. 5 (June 2006): 415–23, e-pub, March 9, 2006.

4. J. H. de Groot, M. A. Smeets, A. Kaldewaij, M. J. Duijndam, and G. R. Semin, "Chemosignals Communicate Human Emotions," *Psychological Science* 23, no. 11 (2012): 1417–24, doi:10.1177/0956797612445317, e-pub, September 27, 2012.

5. M. Oaten, R. J. Stevenson, T. I. Case, "Disgust as a Disease-Avoidance Mechanism," *Psychological Bulletin* 135, no. 2 (2009): 303–321; M. Schaller and L. A. Duncan, "The Behavioral Immune System: Its Evolution and Social Psychological Implications," in *Evolution and the Social Mind*, ed. J. P. Forgas, M. G. Haselton, and W. von Hippel (New York: Psychology Press, 2007), 293–307.

6. P. Prokop, M. Usak, and J. Fancovicová, "Risk of Parasite Transmission Influences Perceived Vulnerability to Disease and Perceived Danger of Disease-Relevant Animals," *Behavioural Processes* 85, no. 1 (September 2010): 52–7, doi:10.1016/j.beproc.2010.06.006, e-pub, June 15, 2010.

7. V. Gallese, L. Fadiga, L. Fogassi, and G. Rizzolatti, "Action Recognition in the Premotor Cortex," *Brain* 119, pt. 2 (April 1996): 593–609.

8. E. J. Moody, D. N. McIntosh, L. J. Mann, and K. R. Weisser, "More than Mere Mimicry? The Influence of Emotion on Rapid Facial Reactions to Faces," *Emotion* 7, no. 2 (May 2007): 447–57.

9. R. Adolphs, "Fear, Faces, and the Human Amygdala," *Current Opinion in Neurobiology* 18, no. 2 (April 2008): 166–72, doi:10.1016/j.conb.2008 .06.006, e-pub, August 12, 2008.

10. A. K. Moskowitz, "'Scared Stiff': Catatonia as an Evolutionary-Based Fear Response," *Psychological Review* 111, no. 4 (October 2004): 984–1002.

11. G. L. Engel, "The Need for a New Medical Model: A Challenge for Bio- medicine," *Science* 196 (1977): 129–136.

12. H. A. Hamann, J. S. Ostroff, E. G. Marks, D. E. Gerber, J. H. Schiller, and S. J. Lee, "Stigma among Patients with Lung Cancer: A Patient- Reported Measurement Model," *Psycho-Oncology* 23, no. 1 (Janu- ary 2014): 81–92, doi:10.1002/pon.3371, e-pub, October 3, 2013; A. Chapple, S. Ziebland, and A. McPherson, "Stigma, Shame, and Blame Experienced by Patients with Lung Cancer: Qualitative Study," *BMJ* 328, no. 7454 (June 19, 2004): 1470, e-pub, June 11, 2004.

Chapter 2: Rapid Response

1. I. J. Mitchell, S. R. Beck, A. Boyal, and V. R. Edwards, "Theory of Mind Deficits Following Acute Alcohol Intoxication," *European Addiction Research* 17, no. 3 (2011): 164–8.

2. A. Day, P. Mohr, K. Howells, A. Gerace, and L. Lim, "The Role of Empathy in Anger Arousal in Violent Offenders and University Students," *Inter- national Journal of Offender Therapy and Comparative Criminology* 56, no. 4 (June 2012): 599–613, doi:10.1177/0306624X11431061, e-pub, Decem- ber 12, 2011.

3. A. A. Marsh and E. M. Cardinale, "Psychopathy and Fear: Specific Im- pairments in Judging Behaviors that Frighten Others," *Emotion* 12, no. 5 (October 2012): 892–8, doi:10.1037/a0026260, e-pub, February 6, 2012.

4. A. S. Smith and Z. Wang, "Salubrious Effects of Oxytocin on Social Stress-Induced Deficits," *Hormones and Behavior* 61, no. 3 (March 2012): 320–30, doi:10.1016/j.yhbeh.2011.11.010, e-pub, December 8, 2011.

5. G. A. Alvares, N. T. Chen, B. W. Balleine, I. B. Hickie, and A. J. Guastella, "Oxytocin Selectively Moderates Negative Cognitive Appraisals in High Trait Anxious Males," *Psychoneuroendocrinology* 37, no. 12 (December 2012): 2022–31, doi:10.1016/j.psyneuen.2012.04.018, e-pub, May 20, 2012.

6. S. Saphire-Bernstein, B. M. Way, H. S. Kim, D. K. Sherman, and S. E. Taylor, "Oxytocin Receptor Gene (OXTR) Is Related to Psychological Re-

sources," *Proceedings of the National Academy of Sciences of the United States of America* 108, no. 37 (September 13, 2011): 15118–22, doi:10.1073 /pnas.1113137108, e-pub, September 6, 2011.

7. D. Agroskin, J. Klackl, and E. Jonas, "The Self-Liking Brain: A VBM Study on the Structural Substrate of Self-Esteem," *PLoS One* 9, no. 1 (January 29, 2014): e86430, doi:10.1371/journal.pone.0086430.

8. C. Cordovil, M. Crujo, P. Vilariça, and P. Caldeira Da Silva, ["Resilience in Institutionalized Children and Adolescents"] [Article in Portuguese], *Acta Médica Portuguesa* 24, Suppl. 2 (December 2011): 413–8, e-pub, December 31, 2011.

9. Devon Maloney, "Our Obsession With Online Quizzes Comes From Fear, Not Narcissism," *Wired* magazine, March 6, 2014, http://www.wired .com/underwire/2014/03/buzzfeed-quizzes.

10. F. Beyer, T. F. Münte, C. Erdmann, and U. M. Krämer, "Emotional Reactivity to Threat Modulates Activity in Mentalizing Network during Aggression," *Social Cognitive and Affective Neuroscience,* e-pub ahead of print, September 20, 2013.

11. D. C. Kidd and E. Castano, "Reading Literary Fiction Improves Theory of Mind," *Science* 342, no. 6156 (October 18, 2013): 377–80, doi:10.1126 /science.1239918, e-pub, October 3, 2013.

12. C. P. Principe and J. H. Langlois, "Children and Adults Use Attractiveness as a Social Cue in Real People and Avatars," *Journal of Experimental Child Psychology* 115, no. 3 (July 2013): 590–7, doi:10.1016/j.jecp.2012.12.002, e-pub, February 8, 2013.

13. N. L. Nelson and J. A. Russell, "Preschoolers' Use of Dynamic Facial, Bodily, and Vocal Cues to Emotion," *Journal of Experimental Child Psychology* 110, no. 1 (September 2011): 52–61, doi:10.1016/j.jecp.2011.03.014, e-pub, April 23, 2011.

14. A. Reijntjes, S. Thomaes, P. Boelen, M. van der Schoot, B. O. de Castro, and M. J. Telch, "Delighted When Approved by Others, to Pieces When Rejected: Children's Social Anxiety Magnifies the Linkage between Self- and Other-Evaluations," *Journal of Child Psychology and Psychiatry* 52, no. 7 (July 2011): 774–81, doi:10.1111/j.1469-7610.2010.02325.x, e-pub, October 6, 2010.

15. M. Bar, M. Neta, and H. Linz, "Very First Impressions," *Emotion* 6, no. 2 (May 2006), 269–78.

16. P. Seabright, *The Company of Strangers: A Natural History of Economic Life* (Princeton, NJ: Princeton University Press, 2010), 14.

Chapter 3: Unexpected Undercurrents

1. S. Rachman, "The Conditioning Theory of Fear-Acquisition: A Critical Examination," *Emotion* 6, no. 2 (May 2006): 269–78; M. Bar, M. Neta, and H. Linz, "Very First Impressions," *Behaviour Research and Therapy* 15, no. 5 (1977): 375–87.

2. C. van der Gaag, R. B. Minderaa, and C. Keysers, "Facial Expressions: What the Mirror Neuron System Can and Cannot Tell Us," *Social Neuroscience* 2, no. 3–4 (2007): 179–222, doi:10.1080/17470910701376878.

3. L. Beaton, R. Freeman, and G. Humphris, "Why Are People Afraid of the Dentist? Observations and Explanations," *Medical Principles and Practice* 23, no. 4 (2014): 295–301, doi:10.1159/000357223, e-pub, December 20, 2013.

4. A. Crego, M. Carrillo-Diaz, J. M. Armfield, and M. Romero, "Applying the Cognitive Vulnerability Model to the Analysis of Cognitive and Family Influences on Children's Dental Fear," *European Journal of Oral Sciences* 121, no. 3, pt. 1 (June 2013): 194–203, doi:10.1111/eos.12041, e-pub, April 19, 2013.

5. X. Gao, S. H. Hamzah, C. K. Yiu, C. McGrath, and N. M. King, "Dental Fear and Anxiety in Children and Adolescents: Qualitative Study Using YouTube," *Journal of Medical Internet Research* 15, no. 2 (February 22, 2013): e29, doi:10.2196/jmir.2290.

6. Ibid.

7. M. L. Goettems, T. M. Ardenghi, A. R. Romano, F. F. Demarco, and D. D. Torriani, "Influence of Maternal Dental Anxiety on the Child's Dental Caries Experience," *Caries Research* 46, no. 1 (2012): 3–8, doi:10.1159/000334645, e-pub, December 8, 2011.

8. J. M. Armfield and L. J. Heaton, "Management of Fear and Anxiety in the Dental Clinic: A Review," *Australian Dental Journal* 58, no. 4 (December 2013): 390–407, quiz 531, doi:10.1111/adj.12118.

9. J. Bowlby, *Attachment and Loss*, vol. 1: *Attachment* (New York: Basic Books, 1968); M. Ainsworth, M. Blehar, E. Waters, and S. Wall, *Patterns of Attachment* (Hillsdale, NJ: Lawrence Erlbaum and Associates, 1978); M. Main and J. Solomon, "Discovery of a New, Insecure-Disorganized/

Disoriented Attachment Pattern," in *Affective Development in Infancy*, ed. T. B. Brazelton and M. Yogman (Norwood, NJ: Ablex, 1986), 95–124.

10. R. D. Goodwin and T. H. Styron, "Perceived Quality of Early Paternal Relationships and Mental Health in Adulthood," *Journal of Nervous and Mental Disease* 200, no. 9 (September 2012): 791–5, doi:10.1097/NMD.0b013e318266f87c.

11. L. Roque, M. Veríssimo, T. F. Oliveira, and R. F. Oliveira, "Attachment Security and HPA Axis Reactivity to Positive and Challenging Emotional Situations in Child-Mother Dyads in Naturalistic Settings," *Developmental Psychobiology* 54, no. 4 (May 2012): 401–11, doi: 10.1002/dev.20598, e-pub August 23, 2011.

12. M. Crosby Budinger, T. K. Drazdowski, and G. S. Ginsburg, "Anxiety-Promoting Parenting Behaviors: A Comparison of Anxious Parents with and without Social Anxiety Disorder," *Child Psychiatry and Human Development* 44, no. 3 (June 2013): 412–8, doi:10.1007/s10578-012-0335-9.

13. S. J. Neill, S. Cowley, and C. Williams, "The Role of Felt or Enacted Criticism in Understanding Parent's Help Seeking in Acute Childhood Illness at Home: A Grounded Theory Study," *International Journal of Nursing Studies* 50, no. 6 (June 2013): 757–67, doi:10.1016/j.ijnurstu.2011.11.007, e-pub, December 2, 2011.

14. S. Rachman, "The Conditioning Theory of Fear-Acquisition: A Critical Examination," *Behaviour Research and Therapy* 15, no. 5 (1977): 375–87.

15. D. Ding, N. L. Bracy, J. F. Sallis, B. E. Saelens, G. J. Norman, S. K. Harris, N. Durant, D. Rosenberg, and J. Kerr, "Is Fear of Strangers Related to Physical Activity Among Youth?," *American Journal of Health Promotion* 26, no. 3 (January–February 2012): 189–95, doi:10.4278/ajhp.100701-QUAN-224.

16. H. Meltzer, P. Vostanis, N. Dogra, L. Doos, T. Ford, and R. Goodman, "Children's Specific Fears," *Child: Care, Health and Development* 35, no. 6 (November 2009): 781–9, doi:10.1111/j.1365-2214.2008.00908.x, e-pub, October 30, 2008.

17. P. Muris, D. Bodden, H. Merckelbach, T. H. Ollendick, and N. King, "Fear of the Beast: A Prospective Study on the Effects of Negative Information on Childhood Fear," *Behaviour Research and Therapy* 41, no. 2 (February 2003): 195–208.

18. Samuel Shem, *The House of God*, reissue ed. (New York: Berkley Trade, 2010).

19. D. Remmerswaal, P. Muris, and J. Huijding, "'Watch Out for the Gerbils, My Child!': The Role of Maternal Information on Children's Fear in an Experimental Setting Using Real Animals," *Behavior Therapy* 44, no. 2 (June 2013): 317–24, doi:10.1016/j.beth.2013.01.001, e-pub, January 28, 2013.

20. J. Huijding, P. Muris, K. J. Lester, A. P. Field, and G. Joosse, "Training Children to Approach or Avoid Novel Animals: Effects on Self-Reported Attitudes and Fear Beliefs and Information-Seeking Behaviors," *Behaviour Research and Therapy* 49, no. 10 (October 2011): 606–13, doi:10.1016/j.brat.2011.06.005, e-pub, June 21, 2011.

21. M. L. Goettems, T. M. Ardenghi, A. R. Romano, F. F. Demarco, and D. D. Torriani, "Influence of Maternal Dental Anxiety on the Child's Dental Caries Experience," *Caries Research* 46, no. 1 (2012): 3–8, doi:10.1159/000334645, e-pub, December 8, 2011.

22. L. Vagnoli, S. Caprilli, and A. Messeri, "Parental Presence, Clowns or Sedative Premedication to Treat Preoperative Anxiety in Children: What Could Be the Most Promising Option?," *Paediatric Anaesthesia* 20, no. 10 (October 2010): 937–43, doi:10.1111/j.14609592.2010.03403.x.

23. C. M. McMurtry, C. T. Chambers, P. J. McGrath, and E. Asp, "When 'Don't Worry' Communicates Fear: Children's Perceptions of Parental Reassurance and Distraction during a Painful Medical Procedure," *Pain* 150, no. 1 (July 2010): 52–8, doi:10.1016/j.pain.2010.02.021, e-pub, March 15, 2010.

24. V. E. Cobham, M. R. Dadds, S. H. Spence, and B. McDermott, "Parental Anxiety in the Treatment of Childhood Anxiety: A Different Story Three Years Later," *Journal of Clinical Child and Adolescent Psychology* 39, no. 3 (2010): 410–20, doi:10.1080/15374411003691719.

25. A. Telford, C. F. Finch, L. Barnett, G. Abbott, and J. Salmon, "Do Parents' and Children's Concerns about Sports Safety and Injury Risk Relate to How Much Physical Activity Children Do?," *British Journal of Sports Medicine* 46, no. 15 (December 2012): 1084–8, doi:10.1136/bjsports-2011-090904, e-pub, July 18, 2012.

Chapter 4: Social Security

1. They were actually the Friedman sisters—Ann Landers was Esther's pen name and Abigail Van Buren was Pauline's pen name; quote from "Twisted Minds Make Halloween a Dangerous Time," *Daily Courier,* October 31, 1995.

2. D. Lewis, "Where Did the Fear of Poisoned Halloween Candy Come From? The Answer, as Always, Is to Blame the Media," Smithsonian .com, October 7, 2013, http://www.smithsonianmag.com/not-categorized /where-did-the-fear-of-poisoned-halloween-candy-come-from-822302 /?no-ist.

3. J. Best and G. Horiuchi, "The Razor Blade in the Apple," *Social Problems* 32, no. 5 (June 1985): 488–99.

4. Joel Best interview, *Los Angeles Times,* November 9, 1989.

5. M. Price and P. L. Anderson, "Outcome Expectancy as a Predictor of Treatment Response in Cognitive Behavioral Therapy for Public Speaking Fears within Social Anxiety Disorder," *Psychotherapy (Chicago, IL)* 49, no. 2 (June 2012): 173–9, doi:10.1037/a0024734, e-pub, October 3, 2011.

6. G. B. Stickler and Department of Pediatrics, Mayo Clinic and Mayo Foundation, "Worries of Parents and Their Children," *Clinical Pediatrics* 35, no. 2 (1996): 84–90.

7. U.S. Department of Justice, "National Incidence Studies of Missing, Abducted, Runaway and Thrownaway Children," October 2002, http://www.missingkids.com/Publications/PDF23A.

8. A. Javor, M. Koller, N. Lee, L. Chamberlain, and G. Ransmayr, "Neuro-marketing and Consumer Neuroscience: Contributions to Neurology," *BMC Neurology* 13 (February 6, 2013): 13, doi:10.1186/1471-2377-13-13.

9. E. Ritvo, J. Q. Del Rosso, M. A. Stillman, and C. La Riche, "Psychosocial Judgements and Perceptions of Adolescents with Acne Vulgaris: Blinded, Controlled Comparison of Adult and Peer Evaluations," *Biopsychosocial Medicine* 5, no. 1 (August 13, 2011): 11.

10. M. M. McDonald, C. D. Navarrete, and M. Van Vugt, "Evolution and the Psychology of Intergroup Conflict: The Male Warrior Hypothesis," *Philosophical Transactions of the Royal Society of London, Series B, Biological Sciences* 367, no. 1589 (March 5, 2012): 670–9, doi:10.1098 /rstb.2011.0301.

11. B. Shaffer and J. Duckitt, "The Dimensional Structure of People's Fears, Threats, and Concerns and Their Relationship with Right-Wing Authoritarianism and Social Dominance Orientation," *International Journal of Psychology* 48, no. 1 (2013): 6–17.

12. K. Nawata and H. Yamaguchi, ["The Role of Collective Victimhood in

Intergroup Aggression: Japan-China Relations"] [Article in Japanese], *Shinrigaku Kenkyu* 83, no. 5 (December 2012): 489–95.

13. J. H. van der Molen and B. J. Bushman, "Children's Direct Fright and Worry Reactions to Violence in Fiction and News Television Programs," *Journal of Pediatrics* 153, no. 3 (September 2008): 420–4, doi:10.1016/j .jpeds.2008.03.036, e-pub, April 28, 2008.

14. D. W. Pryor and M. R. Hughes, "Fear of Rape among College Women: A Social Psychological Analysis," *Violence and Victims* 28, no. 3 (2013): 443–65.

15. H. Rosoff, R. S. John, and F. Prager, "Flu, Risks, and Videotape: Escalating Fear and Avoidance," *Risk Analysis* 32, no. 4 (April 2012): 729–43, doi:10.1111/j.1539-6924.2012.01769.x, e-pub, February 14, 2012.

16. J. Kinsman, "'A Time of Fear': Local, National, and International Responses to a Large Ebola Outbreak in Uganda," *Global Health* 8 (June 13, 2012): 15, doi:10.1186/1744-8603-8-15.

17. G. S. Gould, A. McEwen, T. Watters, A. R. Clough, and R. van der Zwan, "Should Anti-Tobacco Media Messages be Culturally Targeted for Indigenous Populations? A Systematic Review and Narrative Synthesis," *Tobacco Control* 22, no. 4 (July 2013): e7, doi:10.1136/tobaccocontrol -2012-050436, e-pub, August 22, 2012.

18 A. J. Wakefield, S. H. Murch, A. Anthony, J. Linnell, D. M. Casson, M. Malik, M. Berelowitz, A. P. Dhillon, M. A. Thomson, P. Harvey, A. Valentine, S. E. Davies, and J. A. Walker-Smith, "Ileal-Lymphoid-Nodular Hyperplasia, Non-Specific Colitis, and Pervasive Developmental Disorder in Children," *Lancet* 351, no. 9103 (February 28, 1998): 637–41.

19. D. K. Flaherty, "The Vaccine-Autism Connection: A Public Health Crisis Caused by Unethical Medical Practices and Fraudulent Science," *Annals of Pharmacotherapy* 45, no. 10 (October 2011): 1302–4, doi:10.1345 /aph.1Q318, e-pub, September 13, 2011.

20. Retraction in *Lancet* 375, no. 9713 (Feb. 6, 2010): 445.

21. Surveillance, Epidemiology, and End Results Program, "SEER Stat Fact Sheets: Cervix Uteri Cancer," http://seer.cancer.gov/statfacts/html/cervix .html.

22. M. Lemal and J. Van den Bulck, "Television News Coverage about Cervical

Cancer: Impact on Female Viewers' Vulnerability Perceptions and Fear," *European Journal of Public Health* 21, no. 3 (June 2011): 381–6, doi:10 .1093/eurpub/ckq040, e-pub, May 26, 2010.

23. K. Ackerson and S. D. Preston, "A Decision Theory Perspective on Why Women Do or Do Not Decide to Have Cancer Screening: Systematic Review," *Journal of Advance Nursing* 65, no. 6 (June 2009): 1130–40, doi:10.1111/j.1365-2648.2009.04981.x, e-pub, April 3, 2009.

24. V. Graupmann, I. Peres, T. Michaely, T. Meindl, D. Frey, M. Reiser, E. Pöppel, K. Fehse, and E. Gutyrchik, "Culture and Its Neurofunctional Correlates When Death Is in Mind," *Neuroscience Letters* 548 (August 26, 2013): 239–43, doi:10.1016/j.neulet.2013.05.062, e-pub, June 7, 2013.

25. Karl Marx, "A Contribution to the Critique of Hegel's Philosophy of Right," *Deutsch-Französische Jahrbücher,* February 7 & 10, 1844.

26. U. Schjoedt, H. Stødkilde-Jørgensen, A. W. Geertz, T. E. Lund, and A. Roepstorff, "The Power of Charisma—Perceived Charisma Inhibits the Frontal Executive Network of Believers in Intercessory Prayer," *Social and Cognitive Affective Neuroscience* 6, no. 1 (January 2011): 119–27, doi:10.1093/scan/nsq023, e-pub, March 12, 2010.

27. K. E. Vail 3rd, Z. K. Rothschild, D. R. Weise, S. Solomon, T. Pyszczynski, and J. Greenberg, "A Terror Management Analysis of the Psychological Functions of Religion," *Personality and Social Psychology Review* 14, no. 1 (February 2010): 84–94, doi:10.1177/1088868309351165, e-pub, November 25, 2009.

28. Ibid.

Chapter 5: Traversing Together

1. W. W. Ishak, M. Kahloon, and H. Fakhry, "Oxytocin Role in Enhancing Well-Being: A Literature Review," *Journal of Affective Disorders* 130, no. 1–2 (April 2011): 1–9, doi:10.1016/j.jad.2010.06.001, e-pub, July 2, 2010.

2. J. Holt-Lunstad, W. A. Birmingham, and K. C. Light, "Influence of a 'Warm Touch' Support Enhancement Intervention among Married Couples on Ambulatory Blood Pressure, Oxytocin, Alpha Amylase, and Cortisol," *Psychosomatic Medicine* 70, no. 9 (November 2008): 976–85, doi:10.1097/PSY.0b013e318187aef7, e-pub, October 8, 2008.

3. A. Pawlowski, "Firefighters Sing 'Let It Go' to Soothe Girl Stuck in Elevator," TODAY.com, March 24, 2014.

4. P. Duquette, "Reality Matters: Attachment, the Real Relationship, and Change in Psychotherapy," *American Journal of Psychotherapy* 64, no. 2 (2010): 127–51.

5. J. D. Watson and F. H. Crick, "Molecular Structure of Nucleic Acids: A Structure for Deoxyribose Nucleic Acid," *Nature* 171, no. 4356 (April 25, 1953): 737–8.

About the Author

Dr. Joseph Shrand is triple board certified in adult psychiatry, child and adolescent psychiatry, and addiction medicine, and is a diplomate of the American Board of Addiction Medicine. He is also an instructor of psychiatry at Harvard Medical School and the medical director of CASTLE (Clean And Sober Teens Living Empowered), part of High Point Treatment Center in Brockton, MA.

He is the author of *Manage Your Stress: Overcoming Stress in the Modern World* and *Outsmarting Anger: 7 Strategies for Defusing Our Most Dangerous Emotion,* which was the winner of a 2013 Books for a Better Life Award in the Psychology category.

Dr. Shrand helped to design the Independence Academy, the first sober high school on the South Shore of Massachusetts, and currently sits on its steering committee. He teaches psychiatry residents-in-training as a member of the Brockton VA staff and is the medical director of Road to Responsibility, a community-based program that tends to adults with significant developmental disabilities. He is also the founder of Drug Story Theater, Inc., a nonprofit organization that teaches improvisational theater techniques to teenagers in the early stages of recovery from alcohol and other drug addictions.

"Doctor Joe," as he is affectionately called by colleagues and staff, is a nationally recognized psychiatric expert and appears regularly on New England Cable News, where he has been asked to comment on topics ranging from the Boston Marathon bombings to the Newtown tragedy. He was featured in an ABC News series during the 2012 Suicide Prevention Week, and has been quoted in popular magazines and websites such as *Good Housekeeping, Psychology Today, Everyday Health,* and TODAY's section "Today Parents."

Hazelden, a national nonprofit organization founded in 1949, helps people reclaim their lives from the disease of addiction. Built on decades of knowledge and experience, Hazelden offers a comprehensive approach to addiction that addresses the full range of patient, family, and professional needs, including treatment and continuing care for youth and adults, research, higher learning, public education and advocacy, and publishing.

A life of recovery is lived "one day at a time." Hazelden publications, both educational and inspirational, support and strengthen lifelong recovery. In 1954, Hazelden published *Twenty-Four Hours a Day,* the first daily meditation book for recovering alcoholics, and Hazelden continues to publish works to inspire and guide individuals in treatment and recovery, and their loved ones. Professionals who work to prevent and treat addiction also turn to Hazelden for evidence-based curricula, informational materials, and videos for use in schools, treatment programs, and correctional programs.

Through published works, Hazelden extends the reach of hope, encouragement, help, and support to individuals, families, and communities affected by addiction and related issues.

For questions about Hazelden publications,
please call **800-328-9000**
or visit us online at **hazelden.org/bookstore.**

Other titles that may interest you:

The Gifts of Imperfection
Let Go of Who You Think You're Supposed to Be and Embrace Who You Are
BRENÉ BROWN, PH.D., L.M.S.W.

In *The Gifts of Imperfection,* Brené Brown, a leading expert on shame, authenticity, and belonging, shares what she's learned from a decade of research on the power of *Wholehearted Living,* a way of engaging with the world from a place of worthiness.

Order No. 2545 (softcover)
Also available as an e-book and app.

Almost Anxious
Is My (or My Loved One's) Worry or Distress a Problem?
LUANA MARQUES, PH.D., with ERIC METCALF, M.P.H.

It's only human to worry about problems in our lives—but for some of us, obsessing for weeks and months and avoiding social situations due to feelings of panic can become regular habits. If any of these describe you or a loved one, it could be "almost anxiety."

Order No. 4388 (softcover)
Also available as an e-book.

Conquering Shame and Codependency
8 Steps to Freeing the True You
DARLENE LANCER

Learn how to heal from the destructive hold of shame and codependency by implementing eight steps that will empower the real you and lead to healthier relationships.

Order No. 7554 (softcover)
Also available as an e-book.

Hazelden books are available at fine bookstores everywhere. To order from Hazelden, call **800-328-9000** or visit **hazelden.org/bookstore.** For more information about our mobile apps, visit **hazelden.org/mobileapps.**